The DIY Balloon Birthday Bible

...How To Decorate For Birthdays, Picnics, Family Parties, and Any Other Fun Event!

By Sandi Masori, CBA

Edited by Caity Byrne, CBA

This Book Lovingly Dedicated To
Sam Zeiden
1918- 2016

ISBN-13: 978-1534654099
ISBN-10: 1534654097

© 2016 Sandi Masori,
All Rights Reserved

Acknowledgements

First of all I want to dedicate this book to my grandpa, Sam Zeiden. He was always a huge supporter of everything I did. Papa we'll miss you.

Thank you to my family, Mom, Dad, Shor and Sky- You guys mean the world to me. Without your patience and support, I would never be able to achieve any of my dreams.

Thank you to my good friend John Finley. John I literally could not have finished this book without you!

Thank you to my friend and editor Caity Byrne. Without your eagle eye, willingness to travel, late night chats and inspiration, this book would have been a huge jumbled mess!

Thank you to my dear friend Ami Atava. Ames, without your love and shoulder to lean on, I never would have made it through the last few months.

Thank you to my awesome tech crew; Jeff Fu, Quincy Freeman, and GS - you guys were amazing and your dedication and professionalism made sure that these videos got done on time!

Thank you to Kat McDowell for being my first collaboration and making balloon music so much fun.

Thank you to You Tube Space LA, I'm so blessed to have been accepted to the creator program so I could take my videos up a notch.

Thank you to my friend and mentor CJ Matthews. None of my books would have happened if you didn't push me to do the first one.

Thank you to my friend and mentor Clint Arthur. I would not have done any of those TV appearances if it weren't for you!

Thank you to my friend Ken Stillman. I treasure your friendship, willingness to share and your unbelievable talent. Thank you for contributing to this book!

Thank you to Jason M Snyder. You came and saved me when I most needed a pair of skilled hands. This book could not have been without your help.

Thank you to my friend Rachel Porter for letting me use some of her photos in the glossary.

Thank you to my Balloon Business Bootcamp students for having faith in me and trusting me to teach them how to build their business.

And especially thank you to you, my readers. Without you buying my books and watching my videos, I would have no reason to do any of this.

Table of Contents

Acknowledgements iii

THE BEGINNING WHAT YOU NEED TO KNOW BEFORE YOU START 1
How to Make a Balloon Column Frame 2
Lamp Base For Columns 4
How To Make a Balloon Water Weight 6
Building Blocks of Balloons 10
How Are Balloons Affected By Temperature? 15
Balloons Outdoors 17
Balloon Storage 19
Are Balloons Green Enough? 20
Proper Balloon Sizing 22
How to Make a Balloon Sizer Box 24
5 Things to NEVER Do When Planning a Party Outdoors 28
California Balloon Laws 30

PRINCESS/ KNIGHT THEME 33
Unicorn 35
Olaf Door Stopper 43
Frozen Theme Centerpiece with Balloons 47
Frozen Theme Balloon Tower 51
Princess Castle Entryway 57
Giant Balloon Princess 63

CIRCUS / CARNIVAL THEME ... 79
Easy Balloon Clown ... 81
Circus Balloon Tower ... 87
Giant Clown ... 93

RACE CAR / TRAIN THEME ... 101
Chevron Style Balloon Tower ... 103
Racecar ... 107
Traffic Light Tower ... 113

TROPICAL/ UNDER - THE-SEA TEME ... 117
Big Fish ... 119
Octopus ... 125
Seaweed Island ... 137
Life Preserver ... 143
Anchor ... 147
Under the Sea Balloon Photo Frame ... 153
Mini Palm Centerpiece ... 159
Palm Tree Balloon Tower ... 165

GARDEN / FLOWER / SPRING THEME ... 169
Fancy Butterfly ... 171
Butterfly Cloud 9 Balloon Tower ... 179
Giant Balloon Flower Pedestal ... 183
Balloon Flower Arch ... 187

BABY THEME ... 191
Teddy Bear ... 193
Pacifier ... 199
Rubber Ducky ... 203
Baby Shower Teddy Bear Centerpiece ... 207

Welcome Baby Balloon Pedestal.........................213
Balloon Baby Bottle 219

GENERAL DÉCOR 223
Birthday Balloon Totem Pole...........................225
Linky Arch..229
Cupcake Balloon Tower..................................235
Zipper Pattern Balloon Tower 239
Birthday Number Guy....................................243
Whimsical Cow 249
Birthday Color Extravaganza Balloon Tower........255
Squiggle Surprise Pedestal 259
Polka Dot Surprise Balloon Tower.....................265
Electric Balloon Tower 271

INTERACTIVE BALLOONS.............................287
Maraca...289
Balloon Instrument 295
Marshmallow Shooter....................................299
Who Is Sandi Masori?....................................302
Who Is Caity Byrne? 303

Thank You..304

The Beginning — What You Need To Know Before You Start

How to Make a Balloon Column Frame

Materials:
- Piece of wood, square, cut to size needed, painted black
- Flange, painted black
- Threaded pipe
- EMT, coated black

Screw the flange down to your piece of wood. Once you have the flange attached, screw your threaded pipe into the flange. The size is going to depend on what you're doing. I generally use ¾" and then I use ½" EMT.

Then get your EMT. I generally cut them to 7', some cut them to 5'. They come in 10' lengths. Take your pole and simply insert onto your screw. Then put a piece of duct tape where it connects. That's going to make a good, sturdy base plate and pole.

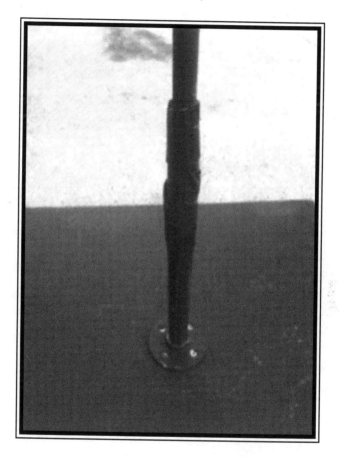

For columns or arches that may go outdoors, or in heavy traffic areas, use a larger piece of wood for a bigger footprint. I recommend 2' by 2'.

If you're trying to make a centerpiece, I would recommend 10" x10" or 12" x 12".

To See Companion Video Go To:
https://youtu.be/hRVvcM7Ytz4

Lamp Base For Columns

*Please note, this is great for columns that will be used indoors, but does not work well for outdoors

Get a floor lamp from anyplace that sells them- i.e. Wal Mart, Ikea, Target...

Cut off the electrical bits

Screw the pieces together. Depending on the size of the design you are making, you may want to use more or fewer pieces. For a centerpiece, 2-3 piece may be sufficient. For the full size columns you might want 5- 6 pieces.

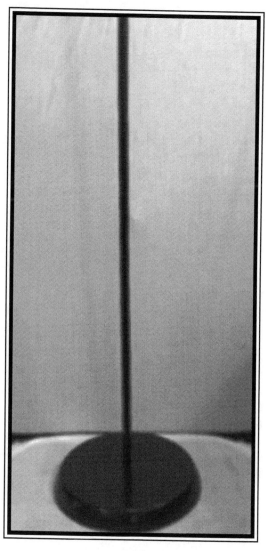

For extra support, use electrical tape to secure connection points. Add balloons ☺

How To Make a Balloon Water Weight

Water weights are very convenient weights. They really help in a pinch, because if you're setting up at an event and you realize that you don't have enough weights with you, ie the client adds more decor on the spot, well you probably have some extra balloons.

First of all, it's really important to double stuff the balloon! I can't stress this enough! By double stuffing the balloon, you ensure that even if there is a little pinhole in the balloon, the water will not leak out.

To double stuff, take two 11" balloons- colors don't necessarily matter, but if you won't be wrapping the balloons in paper, make sure it coordinates with the rest of the decor. Choose which balloon will be the inside balloon. Fold the balloon lengthwise in quarters. This will make a nice little point that will make it easier to stuff one balloon inside the other. Thread the quartered balloon into the other balloon, making sure that the nozzles of the balloons are stacked one on top of the other.

Now, just like making regular water balloons, stretch BOTH nozzles over the water spigot in the sink. Make sure that you are using both nozzles as one, or you will have a big mess. Now fill the bowl of the balloon until it just stretches a little bit- about the size of a baseball (maximum). Do NOT fill the balloon all the way. You just want enough weight to hold down a bouquet, but you want the balloon to stay squishy and strong.

Tie both balloons as if they are one. Some will say that you only need to tie the inner balloon, but I've always found it works better to tie both of them together.

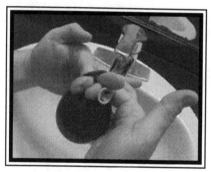 

Now, you have a water weight. You can stop here, and tie the balloon bouquet to it as is, or you can wrap it with paper to make it look more decorative.

Assuming you want to wrap it, you first need to make an attachment point. Take a piece of ribbon, find the center, and tie it around the neck of the balloons. Make a double knot, and set aside.

Take 2-3 sheets of mylar paper, cello paper, tissue paper, or even plastic tablecloth-or any combination thereof. Figure out which color you want to be the base of the weight, and put that one on the bottom. Lay the next piece of paper on top of the first, slightly offset so that it makes a sort of star. Take the 3rd piece and do the same.

If you just drop the water weight in the middle of the papers and wrap it that way, it will look nice, but it will wobble from side to side. This could be a good thing if you want that effect, but if you don't, you need to create a flat surface. To make a flat surface, take something flat and put it on top of the paper. An easy flat object to put on the paper as a base is money- a quarter is a good size, but a nickel will work as well. It's handy and most people have it in their purse or pocket.

After you put the coin on the bottom, drop the weight on top of it. Take the ribbons that you have tied to the balloon in one hand, and with the other, reach under the papers and grab them and bring the corners together- making a little bundle with the weight in the middle. Be careful to make sure that you don't trap the ribbon inside the wrapped weight. Grab the whole thing around the neck, and tie a piece of ribbon around it to secure it. The tighter you tie the ribbon, the nicer it will look.

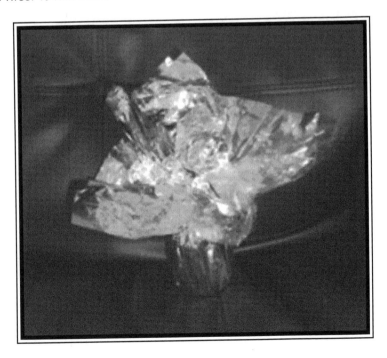

After you tie your helium balloons to the weight you can fluff out the pieces of paper to make it look nice and decorative.

If you are attaching it to clusters of balloons, you don't need to wrap the weight with decorative paper. It's mostly when using helium balloons that you would want to wrap the weights.

> To See The Companion Video Go To:
> https://youtu.be/I5CVCB6cyBI

Building Blocks of Balloons

We're going to talk about the building blocks of balloons, some of the different kinds of balloons and some of the different techniques.

We'll start with Linky balloons. These are so much fun. They've basically got a tail on both ends, so they have your nozzle side so you can blow into it, and then they've got a little tail on the end here so that you can attach things to it or do all kinds of crazy things.

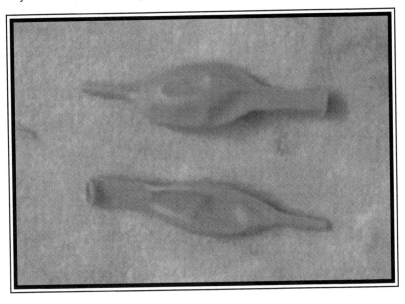

There's a lot of different ways to size your balloons. Another way to size your balloons is to count how many pumps you're doing with your balloon pump, because if you're doing 10 pumps and you do 10 pumps on every balloon then it's going to be the same size. Every Linky balloon that I do 10 pumps on should come out to be the same size.

If you've never used a balloon pump before, when you use the balloon pump you want to put the balloon all the way onto the pump, and then you can't just start pumping because it's going to fly away. What you need to do is actually hold it onto the pump while you pump it. It seems obvious enough, but this is actually one of the most common mistakes and frustrations that I see people making.

Also, make sure that the handle is all the way down, so that you get a full stroke in each direction.

Here's another mistake that I see people making, they'll try to pump it, especially with the 260s, and the balloon will be folded down on the pump, and they're wondering why it's not going. Where's the air going to go, if they've sealed off the chamber? You want to make sure that you're blowing straight into the bowl of the balloon, or in the case of one of the long skinny balloons straight into the tube.

 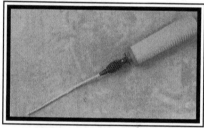

Remember to do a full pump from the bottom all the way to the top.

With Linky balloons we can tie them together in a lot of ways.

Tying two balloons together is called a duplet. The building block of balloon décor is duplets. If you take two duplets and put them together, then you have a quad. This is what we build a lot of our decorations on, quads. Quads are a really important part of balloon decorations.

If you were to take a single balloon and tie it into a quad then you would have a five pack. Five packs can be a huge pain in the butt to work with, but they can be really effective for holding things stably or when you need it to look a little bit rounder.

If you really want it to look round then you're going to want to do a six pack, which I will tell you that the first three six packs that you put onto a pole are a pain in the butt, because one of them always wants to pop up. You've just got to have patience, and you've got to just keep working it and keep playing with it until you get it.

 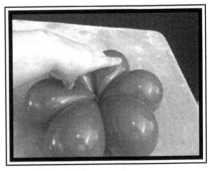

Now let's talk about the non round balloons. There's a lot of different shapes and sizes. We have donuts. We have blossoms. We have hearts. All of those pretty much act the same as round balloons.

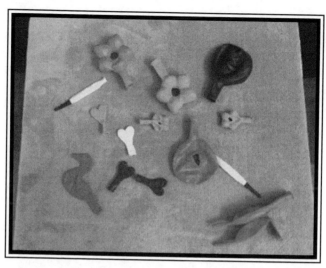

The long balloons act differently. A 160 when fully inflated is approximately 1" wide and 60" long. A 260 when fully inflated is approximately 2" wide and 60" long. A 350 is approximately 3" wide and 50" long. A 646 is approximately 6" wide and 46" long.

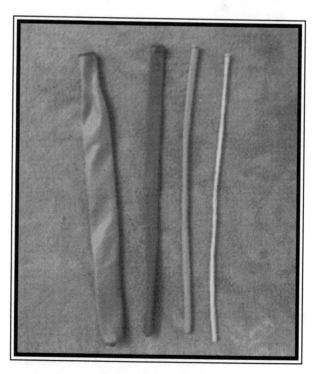

When you fully inflate a balloon and it is very taut you cannot put a twist in it. Usually when we blow up these kinds of balloons before we tie them we give it a burp. What that means is we just let some air out. If I want to use the balloon fully inflated this will work if you only need one twist. If I was going to make a flower, and I needed to have a lot of pressure and have six twists in it, this would be too tight. You want to play with the pressure.

When I'm teaching people in person, I give them a 260, and tell them to inflate it until it pops. That's what I want you to do at home too. The reason is that you need to get the feel for how much the balloon can take, and how much is too little pressure to keep it inflated to the end. Popping a few balloons by overinflating will teach you more about the right way to inflate than any book could.

It's really hard to get a lot of twists in a 646, because they're pretty thick. It's pretty rare that you can do more than one or two twists in one. These are most stable when you're using it as a single balloon or as a single piece. There's a lot of things that we do using this 646s or 660s for the base of a pedestal.

Everybody has a different way to tie it. For the non round balloons I lay it across my hand between my middle finger and my ring finger, and I bring it around the back of my index finger and my middle finger until it crosses. Then I kind of open up my fingers so I can push it through, and I pull it and pull my fingers out. That's how I tie. If you ask five balloon twisters you're going to get five different ways to tie.

The 646 has another really cool property to it. That is that because they're long and heavy. When it's fully inflated, if you put your four fingers and push the end inside, then if you let go these fly off. That's something really fun. Once one of those comes out at a party they're kind of zooming all over the place. Kids love this!

To See The Companion Video Go To:
https://youtu.be/R_fFwVTg--g

How Are Balloons Affected By Temperature?

Has it ever happened to you that you had your balloons set up in the morning for an outdoor event, and around noon all the balloons started popping? Or perhaps your balloons were inflated before the venue turned on the air conditioning, and by the time your party started, all the foils looked like they had lost half of their volume?

Why is this? Most people take their balloons for granted as a decor medium, and rarely think about the science behind their decorations. Floating balloons are filled with a gas called helium. Helium is an inert gas that is lighter than air, (which is why it makes the balloons float). Though helium is not flammable or explosive, it is a gas and therefore reacts quickly to changes in temperature.

If the temperature is higher than it was at the time of inflation, the gas will expand, which can cause the balloon to pop. If the temperature is lower than it was at the time of inflation, the gas will contract and the balloon will look as though it's not full. There's still enough helium to provide the necessary lift to the balloon, so that it will float, but it may look as though it's only half full.

So, now that you know this, what can you do to prevent temperature related balloon disasters? Well, there are a couple of things that can be done:

1. If you expect that the party will be in an air-conditioned room, try to inflate the balloons under the same conditions. Or, if that's not possible, slightly over-inflate the balloons to begin with.

2. If you think that the party will be hotter than the room where you're inflating the balloons, or if you're worried that it will get hotter throughout the day, (a condition that we often have to worry about with balloons in San Diego), then slightly under-inflate your balloons to account for the gas expansion as the temperature rises.

Paying attention to the atmospheric conditions of the room in which you are doing your inflation, and anticipating the temperature of the event will greatly reduce temperature related balloon malfunctions.

Another thing to think about too is how dry the room is. If the room is really dry and carpeted, static electricity can build up and pop the balloons. Spraying the area with a little water can help cut down on balloons popping because of static electricity.

Balloons Outdoors

Summer means picnics, barbeques, pool parties and beach time. And of course, you want to decorate all your parties with balloons.

Balloons are a great medium for attracting attention, adding color and ambiance, and setting the stage. The thing is, balloons outside have different needs and issues than balloons indoors.

First thing to watch out for is heat. Heat can wreak havoc on balloons in many ways. Stay away from dark colors, like black, green, brown, purple, etc., as they absorb heat and can pop. Next, inflate the balloon so that it will float, but leave a little bit of room for the balloon to expand, so it the temperature warms up throughout the day, it won't expand and pop. Inflating 11" balloons to 10.5" is usually enough.

Next thing you have to worry about is wind. As little as four miles an hour is a lot to a balloon. Essentially, the balloon is like a kite or a sail, it can catch the wind and be pushed by it. This means that for free-standing décor, like columns or arches, you want a solid base with a good footprint and weight. Weight alone is not enough, you also need a wide footprint.

Here are some recommendations for strategies to change indoor décor to something that would work better for outdoors:

Arches: Instead of a spiral arch, which is anchored to the ground, it's better to do two columns with wide footprints and have an arch tied into them. The arch can blow down to its anchor point. So, if it's anchored on the ground it can blow all the way down to the ground. If, on the other hand, it's anchored at the 6' mark of a column, it will generally only blow down to that point.

Bouquets: Instead of a bouquet with lots of individual ribbons, which will tangle around each other in the wind, it's better to do décor that is on a single anchor point, like a Cloud 9 or a Topiary kite. Then for extra movement you can put a wide ribbon hanging down to catch the wind and give some rhythm. The single anchor point will work better with the wind, moving from side to side instead of tangling up in itself. Better yet, build a Cloud 9 or Topiary on a base and pole.

Balloon Releases: Check your local city ordinances. Here in San Diego there are restrictions on how many balloons can be released, and releases are never allowed under the flight path or near beaches or bays. Balboa Park doesn't allow balloons of any kind. NEVER do a balloon release with foil balloons. Look up the California balloon laws for more information on that.

Other types of décor that are very effective for outdoors are floating columns, streamers and hi-flyers. Check out the Balloon Utopia website to see examples of this type of décor at

http://www.BalloonUtopia.com

Balloon Storage

Let's talk to you about how to best store your balloons. I'm not talking about balloons that you just brought home from the party and are already inflated. You can store those pretty much however you like. They've already begun their life cycle if you will. The only thing that I would caution you is if you put it down in a cactus, it's going to live a very short life. If you put them in the freezer on the other hand, they'll last just about forever.... (or at least until you take them out of the freezer...)

But, how do you store uninflated balloons? You're playing around with balloons, you're starting to do some stuff, how do you keep your balloons to get the most life out of them? Well, balloons are biodegradable. That means that they breakdown. They do biodegrade, and if you leave them sitting out on your windowsill, you're going to see just how quickly they can breakdown, they change color and start to get brittle – that's the start of the process.

If on the other hand, you store them in a relatively cool, dark area, maybe a closet or in the basement or inside of a box, you're going to get a much longer lifespan out of them because you'll keep the oxidizing process at bay and you'll preserve your balloons for much longer. So the answer to how you'll store your balloons is in a relatively cool dark place. Basically, store the balloons away from heat and sun, and for the longest lifespan, keep them in airtight bags.

Are Balloons Green Enough?

Many people wonder about the environmental impact of balloons. Contrary to popular belief, balloons are one of the most environmentally friendly decor mediums around! Here are a couple of fun facts about balloons and greenness.

Balloons come from the sap of the rubber tree, Heveabrasiliensis, which grows in Malaysia. This sap looks like milk and is shipped to America in large ocean tankers. Once it is removed from the tree, the sap is called latex.

Balloons are biodegradable; they decompose at the rate of an oak leaf under similar conditions.

Balloons are environmentally friendly! Because they are made from the sap of a tree, in order to make more balloons, more trees must be planted!! Does it get any greener than this?

Something that is important to note however, though the latex balloons are completely green, foil balloons are not. Foil balloons do not biodegrade, although being made from metal and plastic, they are recyclable.

If you are planning to use balloons for balloon releases, make sure that you check with the FAA to ensure that you are not in a flight path so as not to cause an accident. Besides getting FAA permission, make sure that the balloons are attached to cotton string which will biodegrade, rather than a poly ribbon, (what most balloon ribbon is made of), which will not biodegrade.

If you are planning on doing balloons outside, make sure that you are following the California balloon laws, even if you are not in California, it's just responsible balloon use.

For indoor parties, make sure that your guests know about responsible balloon use. Make it easy for them to be good citizens, if you are planning to send balloons home with the guests, make sure that they are anchored to a weight so they won't accidentally be released.

With proper thought and care, balloons are one of the most environmentally friendly decor mediums out there!

Proper Balloon Sizing

Sizing a balloon should be a simple thing, right? You just blow and blow until it's full, don't you? Not exactly.... in this article, I'll explain to you exactly how to get the right size for your balloon.

First of all, not all balloons are created equal. Some have the traditional balloon shape, like a tear drop, and some have more of a round shape. For this article, we'll assume the balloons you are using have a traditional shape. The brands of balloons that we like best are Qualatex and Betallic.

The general rule of thumb is that a balloon shaped like a tear drop is properly inflated. If the balloon looks like a light bulb, then it's too full and will probably pop. If it looks like a ball, it's not full enough, and may not float (if filled with helium). Unless you are inflating a 36" giant balloon. Those are supposed to be round.

Sometimes you may want to under-inflate your balloons. If you're building some air-filled decor and it's going to be outside on a hot day, you may want to make those balloons nice and round so that they are fairly squishy and have room to expand.

If you are filling the balloons with helium, you usually will want to fill them to the proper size so that they will float and last the right amount of time.

When would you want to over-inflate the balloons? Well, I guess if you were doing something where having fragile balloons would be an advantage- if you are using water balloons for example, or if you are playing a balloon popping game.

How can you make sure that you size your balloons consistently? Take a box and cut squares out in the sizes you want, i.e. 4", 7", 9", 11" etc. Then inflate the balloon larger than what you think the right size might be. Slowly let the air out until it just clears the hole in the box. Bring it back up and tie it. Repeat with the next balloon. Good looking decor depends on the balloons being sized precisely.

See the chapter on how to make a balloon sizer box for more info.

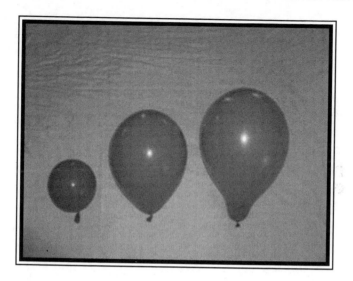

How to Make a Balloon Sizer Box

Materials:
- Box
- Ruler
- Pen
- Box cutter

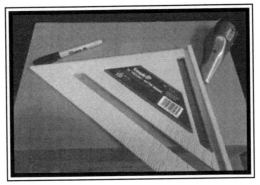

First, get a rigid cardboard box. Then decide what size balloon you are trying to make. Cut a hole to the size that you want to make your balloon. Don't worry about trying to cut a round hole, It's a lot easier to cut a square hole. Just measure to the size you want and cut it out with a box cutter.

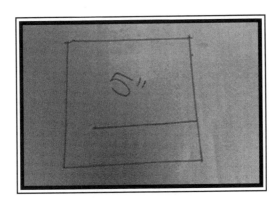

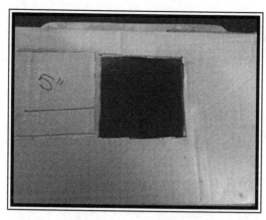

Now, inflate the balloon larger than the hole. Slowly let air out until it just slips through the box. When it just passes through the hole, then you've got the right size. If you let out too much air and there is a gap between the balloon and the square hole, put more air in the balloon and try again.

If you're doing a lot of balloons you might want to have two boxes or have multiple people doing it.

If you have to force it in, it's too big, and if it goes in too easily it's too small. It should just go into the box.

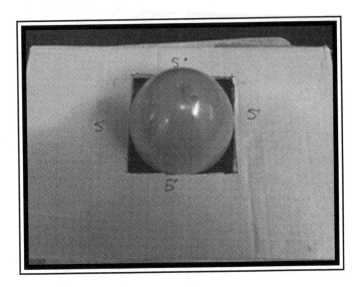

An alternate method to balloon sizing:

Another way to size your balloons is to count how many pumps you're doing with your balloon pump, because if you're doing 10 pumps and you do 10 pumps on every balloon then it's going to be the same size. Every balloon that I do 10 pumps on should come out to be the same size.

Make sure that the handle is all the way down, so that you get a full stroke in each direction.

Here's another mistake that I see people making, they'll try to pump it, especially with the 260s, and the balloon will be folded down on the pump, and they're wondering why it's not going. Where's the air going to go, if they've sealed off the chamber? You want to make sure that you're blowing straight into the bowl of the balloon, or in the case of one of the long skinny balloons straight into the tube.

Remember to do a full pump from the bottom all the way to the top.

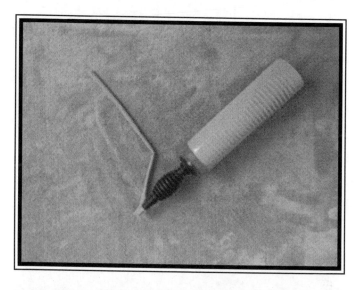

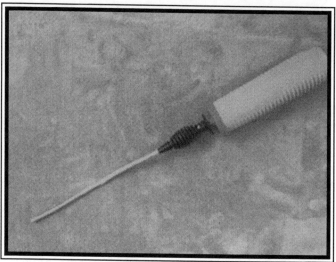

5 Things to NEVER Do When Planning a Party Outdoors

Some basic rules for using balloons outside.

1. Don't let foil balloos go. – When using mylar, or foil, balloons, always have them weighted down. Look at the chapter on California balloon laws, and follow them, even if you don't live in California. A mylar balloon that gets loose can put out an entire electrical grid.
2. Don't Do a Balloon Release without Talking to the FAA first.- Many municipalities have very strict rules about how many balloons you can release without notifying the FAA. A balloon release that gets in the way of a flight path can down a plane. Know the rules for your area.
3. Don't use dark colors – black, brown, purple, blue, green, etc absorb heat, so on a really hot day, these colors are more prone to popping than lighter colors might be.
4. Don't move cold to hot- Inflate the balloons in the environment in which they will be used, going from one temperature to another can cause the gas inside the balloons to contract or expand which could cause the balloon to pop.
5. More weight, the better- it's always better to have a heavier weight and a larger footprint. Stable decorations are happy decorations.

With balloons outside you want to be safe.

You don't want to use dark colors outdoors. These colors are not good for outdoors because when it heats up, when you go from cold to hot, they're going to pop. They expand and they pop. Along those same lines, you want to underinflate. You want them to be squishy.

To help you remember the rules for balloons outdoors, here's The SUN formula:

S – Secure them. Make sure that there's adequate weight.

U – Underinflate. Make them squishy.

N – No helium necessary. If you do it out of air you're going to be able to do more. It'll look better, and it'll better outside.

California Balloon Laws

Did you know that there are special balloon laws in California? Did you even know that there was such a thing as balloon laws?

Here in California we have balloon laws that the rest of the country doesn't have... yet. But even if you're not in California, it's important to know about the balloon laws.

Why, you ask? Imagine that you're giving balloons away at a party and one gets away and floats up into a power line. That balloon could put out the electricity for the entire neighborhood, possibly even an entire grid. Foil balloons are made from a metallic coated plastic, and they conduct electricity. That's what the laws are all about. Below is a quick summary of the California balloon law...

- Never use metallic ribbon on ANY helium filled balloon.

This is for the same reason, metallic ribbon conducts electricity, so if that balloon gets loose, even if it's a latex balloon, and the ribbon wraps around power lines it can put out an entire grid. Never use metallic ribbon on anything that's filled with helium.

- Use balloon weights

All foil balloons have to be anchored to a weight. That weight can be anything, as long as it's heavy enough to hold down the balloon. They make weights in all sizes, styles, and textures. It doesn't have to be fancy. You could also use a slap bracelet. Then the kids could wear it, and then they've got the balloon on their wrist. Sometimes when we don't want the weight to be seen we'll use fishing weights that we get at the hardware store.

Sometimes we'll use flat washers, or water bottles that we've wrapped in paper, even water balloons that we've wrapped in nice paper. The weight can be anything as long as it's heavy enough to hold down the balloon.

Never group foil balloons.

Each balloon has to be anchored by itself.

- Individually anchor each foil balloon.

You can't do a cluster of foil balloons tied together that are helium filled. If it is air filled, you can make columns out of all foil balloons, because air filled balloons don't float. With helium filled balloons, you have to be careful what you're attaching them to and how you're putting them together. You can't group the balloons together and then tie them down to the weight, because if that weight gets cut off now you've got a big group of foil balloons that can get wrapped around power lines. If you're doing a grouping of balloons that's mixed balloons you don't want to tie them together. You want to have your latex balloons arranged, and then bring in your foil balloon, and bring that ribbon all the way down to the weight and tie it onto the weight itself. Better yet, tie each balloon to a small weight individually and cover the weights creatively creating a tablescape. Then your guests can take home balloons easily, as each balloon will already be tied to its own weight.

A place where it really makes a difference is in arches. Those big giant letter balloons are fun to use, but if you're going to make such an arch it has to be against a wall. You wouldn't be able to walk underneath it because once you get your balloons where you want them you then need to go back and tie a ribbon or line from every single letter balloon down to its own weight.

There's a bit more, but that's really the gist of it. It's really important to follow them because loose foil balloons theoretically could put out the lights for a whole neighborhood. In California we almost even lost the right to sell any kind of foil balloons. If we don't use them responsibly, we could lose the fun and excitement that foil balloons can bring to a party. And if it almost happened here, it could happen in other places too...

Princess/ Knight Theme

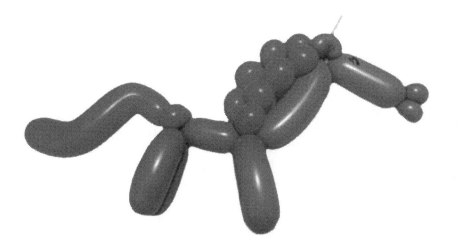

Unicorn

Materials:
- Two 260 balloons
- One 160 balloon

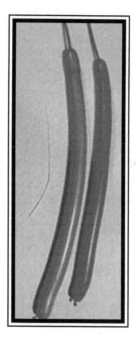

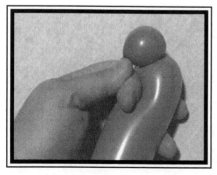

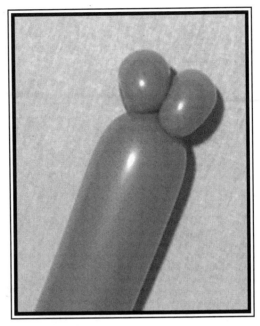

Start with a 260 inflated about three quarters of the way. Use the nozzle to make a pinch twist at the end. Make a second pinch twist. This is the lips.

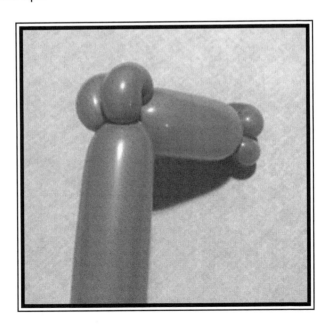

Twist a four-finger-width bubble behind the lips, and make two more pinch twists. These are the ears.

Twist a bubble slightly larger than the head bubble for the neck.

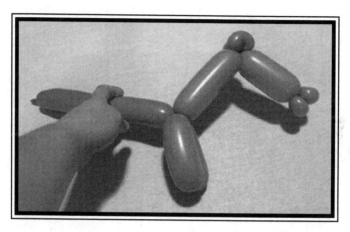

Twist two bubbles for the legs, securing them at the base of the neck.

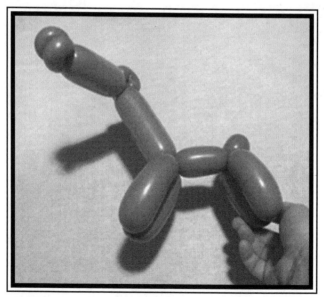

Twist another longer bubble for the back, and then two more legs to match the front.

Feed the end piece through the back legs a few times to secure.

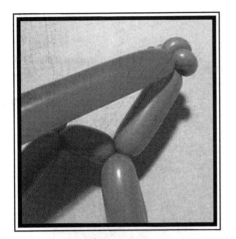

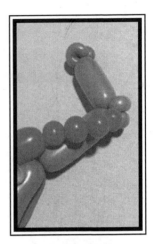

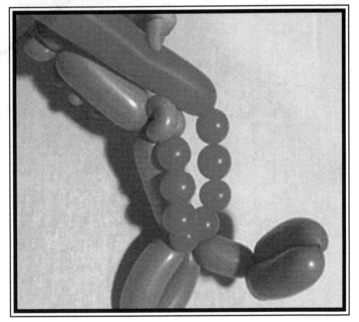

Take the second 260 and wrap the nozzle around the ears.

Make a four bubble chain. Make sure that you maintain control of the first and last bubble at all times. You always want to twist in the same direction and the same number of rotations.

After the final bubble in the chain, twist into the neck.

Repeat the chain back up the neck and wrap around the ears again.

Take the four bottom bubbles and wrap them around each other.

Make a third bubble chain of four down the neck. Wrap into the neck and around the legs to secure.

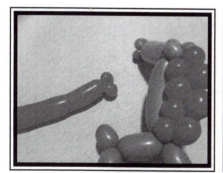 

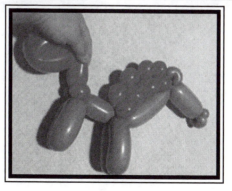

Remove excess without deflating. Release a little of the pressure. You need to get two twists into this balloon part. Tie off. This will be your tail.

Make two pinch twists into the end you removed.

Take the two pinch twists and push them between the back legs, bringing them up to the top. Wrap around the top of the legs to secure.

Remove the excess piece of the first 260.

Give the tail a gentle S curve and squeeze to move the air.

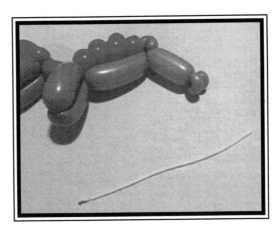

Take your 160 and put a puff of air into it. This is your horn.

Wrap the 160 around the ears, arranging so that the horn sticks up between the ears.

Wrap the end around to secure. Remove the excess 160.

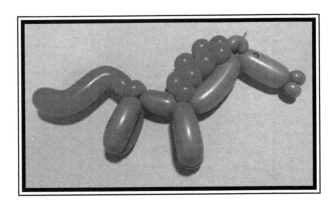

Use a marker to draw on eyes.

To See The Companion Video Go To:
https://youtu.be/YqVXq9y6-tc

Olaf Door Stopper

Materials:
- Water weight
- Olaf-shaped mylar balloon
- Five 11" balloons, inflated to 8"
- Five 11" balloons, inflated to 6"
- Five 5" balloons, inflated to 4"
- Uninflated 260

Tie the 8" balloons into duplets. Add a third balloon into one of the duplets to make a three pack. Twist the two sets of balloons together to make a five pack. Do the same with the 6" balloons.

Twist both five packs together. Once you've done that, bring the 6" balloons up on top of the 8" balloons. This creates a pocket in the middle underneath.

Create a five pack with the 4" balloons. Take one of the nozzles, and figure 8 it into the other five packs. Arrange the balloons on top so that the 4" balloons are nestling into the 6" balloons.

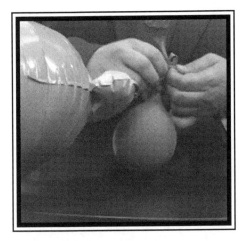

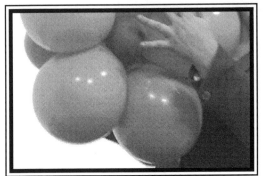 

Tie your uninflated 260 to the nozzle of the Olaf balloon using a lark's head knot. Pull it tight.

Tie the water weight to the same 260 a few inches from Olaf. You don't want too much space or it will be too loose when put into the stack of five packs.

Place Olaf at the top of the stack of five packs and stretch the water weight down so that it nestles into the little pocket at the bottom.

To See The Companion Video Go To:
https://youtu.be/JHPYcRq806c

Frozen Theme Centerpiece with Balloons

Materials:
- One Bubble Balloon, Frozen themed
- One 260, uninflated
- Water weight
- Four 11" balloons, inflated to 6"
- Four 11" balloons, inflated to 5"

Take the 6" balloons and tie them into duplets. Twist the duplets together to make a quad. Do the same with the 5" balloons.

Twist the two quads together. Arrange it so that the 5" balloons are on the top.

Make a lark's head knot in the 260. Pull the nozzle end of the bubble balloon into the loop of the knot and pull both ends of the 260 to tighten.

Tie the other end of the 260 to the water weight, about a 3 finger width from the bubble balloon.

Stretch the 260 into the base of quads so that the bubble balloon rests on top and the water weight is on the bottom.

If it is a little wobbly, wrap the water weight around one of the bottom 6" balloons to tighten it.

To See The Companion Video Go To:
https://youtu.be/AB-ij0m0eGk

Sandi Masori, CBA

Frozen Theme Balloon Tower

Materials:
- Base plate and pole
- Frozen-themed mylar balloon
- Eight 11" round balloons, inflated to 9", tied in a quad, light blue
- Eight 11" round balloons, inflated to 6", tied in a quad, light blue
- 5" round balloons, fully inflated, tied in quads, light blue
- Four 260 balloons, inflated with a small tail, white

Wrap your 9" quad around the bottom of the pole.
Wrap the 6" quad on top of that. Next wrap in a 5" quad.

Continue wrapping the 5" quads up the pole. Make sure you leave enough room at the top of the pole to mirror the bottom.

When you reach the top wrap in a 6" quad followed by a 9" quad.

Use an uninflated 260 to attach the mylar balloon to the top of the pole. Make sure that you are not tying over the valve of the mylar balloon.

Tie your 260s end to end into a long chain.

Work the middle knot of the 260 chain into the column under the second layer from the top.

Take one side of the 260s and spiral them down the column to the bottom. Use the tail piece to wrap it into the bottom quads to secure it. Do the same with the other 260s.

Trim off any excess ends.

To See The Companion Video Go To:
https://youtu.be/9srYXsLF8Os

NOTES

Princess Castle Entryway

Materials:
- Base plate and pole
- 11" balloons, inflated to 8", tied in quads, pink
- Five 16" balloons, inflated to 12", gold
- Four 11" balloons, inflated to 9.5", tied in quad, gold
- Water weight
- 260 balloons, gold

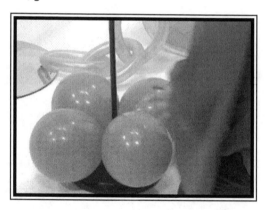

Begin packing the pole at the base with the 8" quads. Continue up the pole, leaving about a 1.5' at the top of the pole for the turret.

Make a quad with four 12" gold balloons and wrap at the top of your column. Next wrap on the 9.5" gold quad.

Take your last 12" gold balloon and tie it into the top quad of your column.

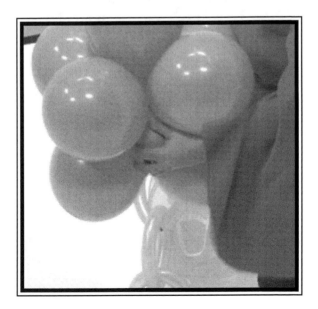

Twist together two more 8" quads. Tie the water weight into the group of balloons you just made so that it nestles into the center.

Now you are going to make your chain link. Take a gold 260 and inflate with a hand pump two pumps. Tie it into a circle. Take a second 260 and inflate two pumps, feed it through the first 260 and tie into a circle. Continue this process to make your chain. Trim the ends. Don't cut the extra off the first and last one, because that is what you will use to tie them on.

Tie one end of your chain to the top of the two 8" quads with the water weight.

Tie the other end of the chain into the top of your column.

Repeat the process for a second column and decide how far apart you want to place them. For a knights castle make it in silver and purple.

To See The Companion Video Go To:
https://youtu.be/pqXDwMVx7Pc

Giant Balloon Princess
By Ken Stillman

Materials:
- Six White 646 balloons, fully inflated, 38 inches long
- Six Blue 646 balloons, fully inflated, 42 inches long
- White 646 balloon, partially inflated
- Twelve White 6" linky balloons, fully inflated
- One 16" Blue round balloon
- One 15" White heart balloon
- Two ½" small rubber balls
- Two Blush 350 balloon, inflated with a burp
- Four White 350 balloons
- Two White 260 balloons
- Three White 160 balloons
- Two White 5" hearts, inflated
- One Blue 646, inflated 10" and burped
- Four Yellow 350 balloons, inflated

Fully inflate the 646 balloons and then let air out of the nozzle end until they are the length you need.

Tie the 646 balloons into duplets, so that you have three of each color. Wrap two blue duplets around each other. Twist in the third one as well. Do the same thing with the white duplets.

Twist a bubble in the end of the partially inflated white 646. Twist that bubble into the center of the white 646s. When you finish you should have something like the spokes on a wagon wheel.

Squeeze the air down in the partially inflated 646 and twist a 4" bubble. Taking three balloons on the top and three on the bottom, wrap the blue 646s around the twist you just made. Wrap the end of the partially inflated 646 completely around and bring it back up to the top. You now have a set of blue spokes 4" away from your white spokes.

Now you're going to make the hem of the dress. Tie your 12 linky balloons together end to end. Tie the ends together to create a circle.

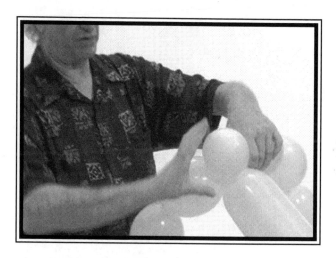

Start with the white 646 spokes of your dress. Squeeze the end and twist as close to a perfect ball as you can. Attach that between two of the linky balloons in the dress hem. Repeat with the next white 646, skipping two linky balloons in between. Continue around the hem in this manner, connecting to every other space between linky balloons.

You want to make sure that your balls are pretty much the same size every time.

Look through the hem of the skirt from the bottom and adjust the balloons so that they are evenly spaced.

Now you are going to do the same thing with the blue 646s. You want to twist the bubbles on the end the same size as the others, and then wrap them in every other linky balloon, between where you twisted in the white 646s.

Deflate the partially inflated white 646 that is sticking up from the top of the skirt and wrap the excess balloon around the blue 646s to secure. This is also the place to tie in if any of your 646s pop.

Place the hem of the skirt on the floor and press down on the top, so that everything goes into place and the bottom flattens out and is stable.

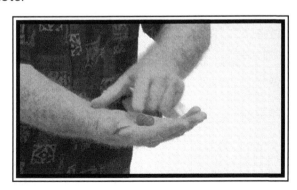

Now you're going to make the bodice. Place the two rubber balls into the blue 16" balloon. This gives you a way to create a heart out of a 16" balloon.

Fold the 15" heart and stick it into the nozzle of the 16" balloon. Inflate the heart balloon, and the round 16" will take on the shape of the heart. Tie the heart balloon to secure. Do not tie the blue in with it.

You want the balls to be at the sides of the heart where the arms are going to be attached. Just use your finger and thumb to roll the ball to where you want it.

Now you are going to attach the arm. Pull up on one of the balls and twist. Take a blush 350 and wrap it around the ball. Squeeze some of the air down in the 360 and make a small soft bubble. Make a pinch twist here to become the shoulder. Do the same to the other side with a second blush 350.

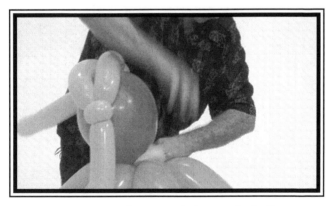

Cross the arms across the top of the neck. Pull one arm across, squeeze a little air out, and twist it around the shoulder. Do the same with the other arm.

You can now attach the bodice to the dress. Use the uninflated white 646 to wrap around the nozzle of the blue 16" balloon and tie it in. Cut off the excess.

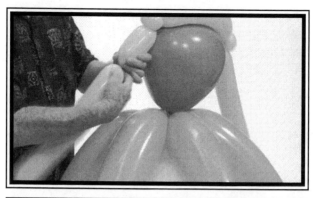

Come down about 4" from the shoulder and twist. Deflate the rest of the arm balloon and tie off. Match the other arm as best you can.

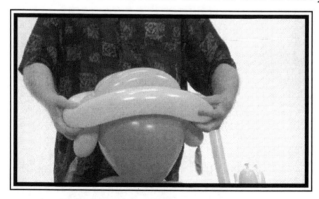

Take a fully inflated white 350 and stretch it. This is the collar, and you want it to wrap completely around the top of the bodice. Twist bubbles on each end of the 350 and twist them together. Test the fit around the bodice. You want it to fit tightly and securely over the top of the shoulders. Once you have the fit you need deflate the small bubbles on the ends and tie them securely. Place the 350 over the shoulders. You can put the split in either the front or the back.

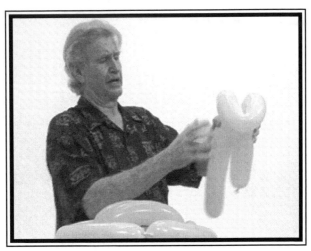

Take an inflated white 350. Fold it in half and squeeze. This will give you a V effect. This is to give the hourglass look to your princess. While it is folded in the V, squeeze about 4" from each side of the point and bend. It will look like handlebars.

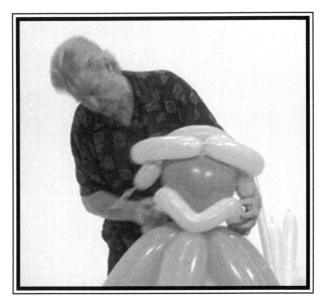

Bring that around the waist, placing the point of the V between two blue 646s. Bring it in as tightly as you can. Twist together in the center of the back. Deflate the excess. Make sure you wrap one deflated end around between the 350 and the bodice before tying the ends together to ensure that it stays tight.

Tie an inflated white 350 to each arm. These will be the gloves. Trim off any excess ends.

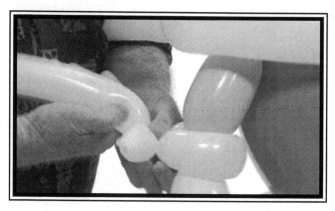

Now you're going to make the top of the glove. Take a white 260, twist a small bubble, and wrap the balloon around the top of the glove. Twist the small bubble around the balloon to secure. Remove the excess 260, keeping it inflated. Bring the uninflated part of the top of the balloon up underneath the glove cuff. Deflate the small bubble you twisted first, and tie the ends together.

Use the piece of the 260 that you kept inflated to make the top of the other glove. Do the same thing you did on the first side, making sure the tops of the gloves are the same size. You do not need to keep the excess 260 inflated after the second glove cuff.

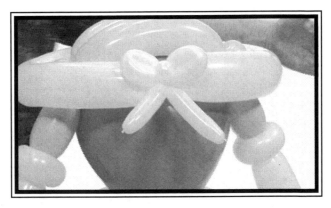

Take an inflated white 160 and twist a 5" bubble, followed by a loop twist. Do another loop twist the same size. Now do a pinch twist. This will be the center of the bow for the collar of the dress. Bring the end down and try to match the size of the first bubble. Remove any excess and tie off.

Push your bow down into the front of the collar where your knot is. Put the pinch twist and loops over the top and the 5" bubbles underneath. You can do the same thing with the sleeves.

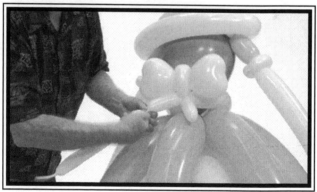

Tie the two white 5" hearts into a duplet. Take another inflated 160 and twist a 6" bubble. Wrap the 160 around where the 5" hearts are tied together and then twist the 160 to itself where you made the initial bubble. You don't want to wrap the hearts into the twist. Make the ends of the 160 the same length, remove the excess and tie off.

Place the bow you've just made into the back of the dress at the waist the same way you did with the bow at the collar.

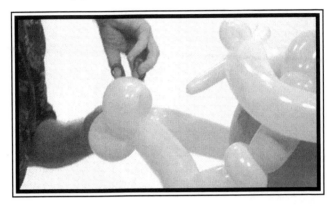

Make some elbows by coming down about 2" from the cuff of the glove and squeezing to make a bend. Do the same on the other side.

Measure her forearms and twist the two arms together at that point. Make two loop twists, one in each balloon, to be her hands. Remove the excess balloon and tie the ends together. Trim off any excess.

Now you are going to make the head. Trim the end of the 10" blush 646.

Tie the yellow 350s into duplets. Twist the duplets together. These will be her hair. Measure a 12" bubble in one of the 350s. Do the same with the other three 350s and twist them all together.

The DIY Balloon Birthday Bible

Take two of the ends of the 350s and measure another 12". Twist them together. Bring them up to the top and feed the ends through the first four bubbles you made. You now have a cluster of six 12" bubbles.

Turn so that the longer ends are at the top. Those are going to be her bangs. The shorter ones will be used to tie her head onto the body.

Open up the yellow balloons a bit, and place the blush head balloon into the cavity you've created.

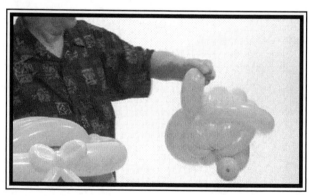

Twist a small bubble at the bottom of the blush balloon for her neck. Deflate one of the shorter yellow ends. Wrap the deflated end around the neck bubble. Bring it back and wrap it around the other yellow balloon, hiding the rest in the back.

Twist a small bubble in the remaining shorter yellow piece. Deflate the rest and tie off. Twist the small bubble up into the hair to hide it.

Take the top yellow balloons for the bangs and bring them down in the front of the head and squeeze. Bring them down the sides of the face and tie them together in the back of the head.

Remove any excess balloon and tie the ends together. You can hide this join with a flower or something similar on the back of the hair.

Slip the neck bubble in between the two blush bubbles at the top of the bodice that make the shoulder blades.

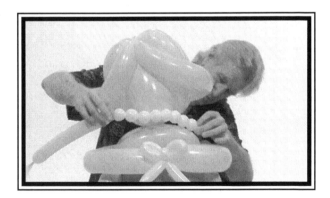

Twist a series of eight or nine bubbles in a white 160. Wrap this necklace around where the head and neck join. Tie the ends together and remove any excess. This will help keep the head from rocking.

If you need to secure the head more take an uninflated blush balloon, tie it to the shoulder. Bring it up to the neck and wrap it around, and then bring it down and tie it to the opposite shoulder.

You can place a heart balloon or flowers or something similar into the hands.

To See The Companion Video Go To:
https://youtu.be/ZtVAiM49Jzg

To See More Of Ken Stillman's Awesome Designs, Check Out His Instructional Site
Http://www.BalloonClick.com

Circus / Carnival Theme

Easy Balloon Clown

Materials:
- Four 11" balloons, inflated to 9", tied in quad, blue
- Four 11" balloons, inflated to 7", tied in quad, blue
- Water weight
- Four 646 balloons, inflated with a 2" tail, tied in quad, blue
- Four 646 balloons, inflated with a 2" tail, tied in quad, red
- Two 350 balloons, fully inflated, tied in duplet, red
- Clown face mylar balloon
- Four 5" balloons, inflated to 3", tied in quad

Twist the 9" and 7" quads of 11" balloons together. Arrange so that the 7" balloons sit on top of the 9" balloons.

Wrap the nozzle of the water weight into the quads so that the weight is centered in the bottom, and tie it to one of the top balloons.

Wrap the blue 646 quad between the two round quads, and then pull it up so that the balloons are standing up.

Place the red 646 quad so that it is sitting in the center and sticking out between each blue 646.

Tie the nipple ends of the blue 646s together.

Do the same with the red 646s; bring the ends up and tie the nipples together.

Take the 350 duplet and feed it through the red 646s and tuck it up into the top. Bend and squeeze each one. These are the arms.

Make a little loop at the end of each 350 for the hands.

Use an uninflated 260 to tie the mylar balloon to the top of the body. You may need to move the arms down while tying and then bring them back up when finished.

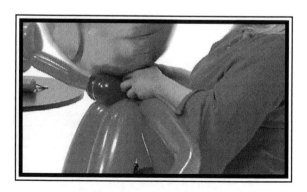

Take your quad of 3" and wrap it at the base of the mylar balloon to stabilize it.

To See Companion Video Go To:
https://youtu.be/zMqfcbYi6vg

NOTES

Circus Balloon Tower

Materials:
- Base plate and pole
- Eight 11" round balloons, inflated to 7.5", tied in quads
- Eight 11" round balloons, inflated to 6", tied in quads
- Eight 5" round balloons, fully inflated, tied in quads
- 3' round balloon
- Eight 260 balloons, fully inflated and burped

Wrap a quad of 7.5" balloons at the base of the pole.

Wrap a 6" quad above the first set.

Next, wrap a 5" quad around the pole.

Wrap a quad of 7.5" balloons at the top of the pole.

Wrap a 6" quad under the 7.5" balloons.

Tie the 260 balloons into duplets. Make a quad of the 260s.

Insert the quad of 260s between the 5" and 6" balloons at the base of the pole, so that one 260 balloon comes up between each of the 5" balloons.

Spiral two of the 260 balloons together. Twist together at the end.

Wrap the spiral around the pole.

Use a quad of 5" balloons to secure the twisted 260s to the pole.

Follow along the curve of the spiraled 260s with the third and fourth 260s, wrapping them up the pole and twisting them into the quad of 5" balloons.

Tie another group of four 260s into duplets and join them in a quad.

Wrap this quad around the pole at the 5" quad in the middle, so that one 260 balloon comes up between each of the 5" balloons.

Repeat the spiral of 260s up the rest of the pole, maintaining the same pattern as the bottom half. Wrap into the balloons at the top to secure.

Use scissors to deflate 260 ends, and wrap the excess around the top round quads in a figure eight to secure. Repeat will all the extra end pieces, including those in the middle.

This is your base column.

Use an uninflated 260 to attach the 3' balloon to the top of the column.

To See The Companion Video Go To:
https://youtu.be/W15AdG-7oFQ

Giant Clown

Materials:

- Base plate and pole
- Two 16" balloons, inflated to 11", blue, duplet
- Two 11" balloons, inflated to 7.5", red, duplet
- Two 5" balloons, inflated to 4", red, duplet
- Four 11" balloons, inflated to 8", red, quad
- Four 11" balloons, inflated to 9.5", red, quad
- Four 11" balloons, fully inflated, red, quad
- Four 16" balloons, inflated to 13", red, quad
- Four 16" balloons, inflated to 14", yellow, quad
- Four 16" balloons, inflated to 13", yellow, quad
- Four 16" balloons, inflated to 12", yellow, quad
- Four 11" balloons, fully inflated, yellow, quad
- Four 16" balloons, inflated to 12", blue, quad
- Twelve 260 balloons, six colors, fully inflated and burped
- Eight 5" balloons, mostly inflated, green, quads
- Two 5" balloons, mostly inflated, white
- One 3' balloon, white
- Two 5" balloons, slightly inflated, blue
- Sticky tabs
- One 5" balloon, slightly inflated, yellow
- One 260 balloon, partially inflated, red
- Twelve 260 balloons, inflated in curlicues, six colors

Create a quad with a duplet of blue 11" balloons and red 7.5" balloons.

Wrap this quad at the base of the pole, arranging so that the two blue balloons are in the front, and the red are in the back.

Take a duplet of 4" red balloons and wrap them to the pole above the 7.5" red balloons, so that it brings the back to the same height as the front.

The larger blue balloons will be the clown's feet.

As you wrap up the pole, you are going to gradually go up in size of balloons. Begin with an 8" red quad above the group of balloons at the bottom of the pole. Next, wrap on a 9.5" quad of red balloons. Next comes a quad of 11" red balloons, then a quad of red 13" balloons. This is the clown's legs.

Now you are going to start on the top.

Wrap a 14" yellow quad onto the pole. This is the waist, the largest part, and now you will begin going down again in balloon size. Wrap on a yellow 13" quad, then a 12" quad. Then wrap on a 11" yellow quad.

Finish packing the column with a 12" blue quad. This is your collar.

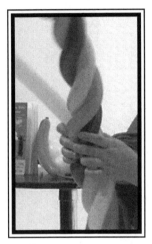

The arms are created with six 260s, one of each color. Tie the 260s into duplets and twist them together to create a six pack.

Take two of the 260s in the group of six and twist them together to create a spiral. Twist at the end to secure.

Take a third balloon from the group and twist it around the first two, following the curve of the spiral you created. Twist at the end to secure. Repeat this until all six balloons are spiraled together.

Once finished you can tighten the spiral by grabbing each end and twisting opposite directions.

Repeat the process of spiraling the six 260s to create the second arm. If the leftover balloon ends at the back of the arm are too long deflate and tie off.

Take an uninflated 260 and tie to the back end of each arm to join them together.

Place arms onto the column between the top blue quad and the second yellow quad, stretching the uninflated quad in the center so that one arm rests on each side of the column.

Tie the single white 5" balloon to one of the 5" green quads to make a quint. Tie the quint onto the end of one of the arms. This becomes a ruffle and the clown's hand. Repeat on the other side.

Now start on the head.

Two slightly inflated blue 5" balloons will be the eyes. Trim the nozzles. Place the eyes onto the 3' white balloon using sticky tabs.

Attach a slightly inflated 5" yellow balloon to the 3' balloon with sticky tabs for the nose.

Use a piece of partially inflated red 260 for the mouth, tie off the end and cut off the excess. Bend into a curve for a smile. Attach to the face with sticky tabs.

Now make the hair.

Tie together the 12 curlicues.

Another way to take curlicues is to take a fully inflated 260 and wrap it around your hand or arm. It's very important that it's a little bit squishy. Gently squeeze some pressure in and out. It's not going to be as tight as ones inflated as curlicues, but you can get a nice curve.

Take your bunch of curlicues and make a slightly flat spot to attach to the top of the head. Make sure you are securing at least four of the curlicue balloons to the head. It's okay if it is not perfect.

Now uncurl some of the curlicues so that they are sticking out.

Tie an uninflated 260 to the nozzle of the 3' balloon and tie it to the top of the clown body. Make sure to crisscross the 260 through at least the top two quads to secure the head.

Now is the time to adjust the arms the way you want them. You can use sticky tabs or glue to secure the arms if you want them in an exact position.

To See The Companion Video Go To:
https://youtu.be/OhxwKKK0CNU

NOTES

Race Car / Train Theme

Chevron Style Balloon Tower

Materials:
- Base plate and pole
- 11" balloons in two colors, tied in quads

The first thing to decide is what color is your first arrow going to be.

Wrap your first quad onto the pole at the bottom. Whatever color you are starting with, you want that to be the color of the "wings"- the two balloons on the side. The center one is going to be the odd color out.

The next quad is going to be a solid color in the color you want the arrow. Wrap it above the first quad.

Take another quad that is two of each color. Wrap it onto the pole with your arrow color in the center this time.

The next quad you wrap on should be a solid color of the second color.

Wrap in a two and two quad, putting the second color in the center.

Wrap in a solid quad of the first color.

Wrap in a two and two quad with the first color in the center. Continue wrapping up the pole following this design.

This design will look different depending on which side of the pole you are looking at.

To See The Companion Video Go To:
https://youtu.be/qy7JfnB6W8w

Racecar

Materials:
- Base plate and pole
- Eight 11" balloons, inflated to 9", black and white, quads (2 balloons each color)
- Eight 11" balloons, inflated to 7", black and white, quads (2 balloons each color)
- Mylar balloon
- Two 260 balloons, inflated in curlicues, red

Wrap a 9" quad onto the bottom of the pole, alternating colors.
Wrap a 7" quad above the first, alternating colors again.

You now want to mirror this on the top. Start with a 9" quad at the top of the pole, alternating colors, and wrap a 7" quad below it.

If you are making a centerpiece, use slightly smaller balloons, 7" and 4".

Tie an uninflated 260 to the Mylar balloon. Make sure not to crush the valve, because that could create a slow leak.

Use the 260 to tie the Mylar balloon to the top of the pole, wrapping it around and through the quads at the top to secure.

To create the curlicue, fully inflate a 260 balloon and let all the air out. Wrap the 260 around your fingers, being careful not to twist it. Inflate the 260 while it is wrapped around your fingers.

Take your two curlicues and tie them together.

Wrap the duplet of curlicues between the bottom two quads, arranging so that the 260s come up between the 7" balloons.

Wrap one of the curlicues around the pole in a spiral. Repeat with the second.

Twist the two ends of the curlicues and tie them together. Loop the tied ends over one of the 9" in the quad above to secure.

To See The Companion Video Go To:
https://youtu.be/uh87wer0P_8

NOTES

Traffic Light Tower

Materials:
- Base plate and pole
- Twenty-two Black 11" balloons, inflated to 7.5", tied in duplets
- Two Red 11" balloons, inflated to 8", tied in duplets
- Two Green 11" balloons, inflated to 8", tied in duplets
- Two Yellow 11" balloons, inflated to 8", tied in duplets
- Four Black 11" balloons, inflated to 10", wrapped in a quad
- Four Black 11" balloons, inflated to 6", wrapped in a quad
- Four Black 5" balloons, inflated to 4", wrapped in a quad
- Four Black 260s, inflated with a small tail, tied in duplets

Twist two black duplets together into a quad. Wrap that onto the top of the pole.

Twist together the red duplet and a black duplet into a quad. Wrap it onto the pole directly beneath the black quad. You want the red balloons to be on opposite sides of the pole, so that you can have a two-sided traffic light.

Twist together two black duplets into a quad and wrap them onto the pole directly under the red and black one.

Now twist together the yellow duplet and a black duplet. Wrap this onto the pole, making sure that the yellow balloons line up under the red balloons.

Now wrap another quad of black balloons onto the pole.

Now twist together the green duplet and a black duplet. Wrap it onto the pole, lining the green balloons up with the red and yellow ones.

Wrap another black quad onto the pole under the green and black balloons. This completes the top of the traffic light.

Take your 10" black quad and wrap it at the base of the pole. Wrap the 6" quad directly on top of it. Wrap the 4" quad on top of that.

Wrap together the two duplets of 260s to make a quad.

Feed the quad in between the balloons at the bottom quad of the stop light, under the green balloons. You want to have one 260 coming down the pole between each balloon of the bottom quad.

Take two of the 260s and spiral them together. Wrap the spiral around the pole, following the spiral you just created.

When you get to the bottom, wrap it into the 5" balloons.

Wrap the third 260 around the pole, following the spiral and twisting in at the bottom. Do the same with the final 260.

Deflate any excess 260 ends, wrapping the ends into the base quads to secure.

To See The Companion Video Go To:
https://youtu.be/PITY_FlrBFM

Tropical/ Under-The-Sea Teme

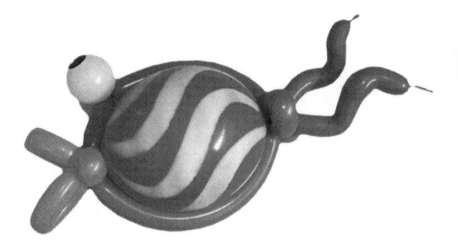

Big Fish

- One 12" Linky balloon
- Two 5" eyeball balloons, tied in duplet
- Three 260 balloons

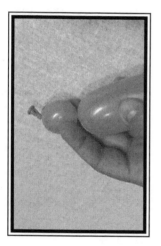 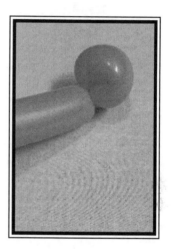

Inflate your first 260 about half way.

Grab the nozzle of the 260 and make a small loop about the size of your thumb, squeeze and twist, and pull the nozzle through to lock it.

 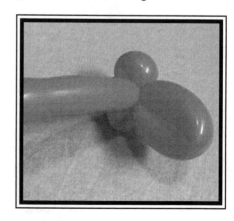

Keep hold of the nozzle while making a second loop to match the first.

Make a third loop that is about a third larger than the first two. At this point you can let go of the nozzle.

Twist a fourth loop that matches the size of the third loop. These are your lips.

Wrap the end of the 260 around a few times to make sure it is secure. Remove the excess.

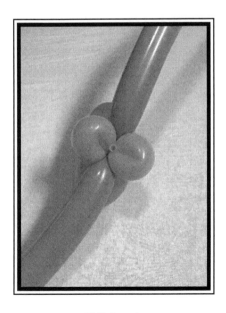

Inflate the second and third 260s with about a two inch tail. Tie them together into a duplet.

Take the lips you made and wrap them around where you tied the two 260s together. Arrange so that the smaller loops are on the sides, and the two larger loops are in the center to make the lips.

Take the Linky balloon and wrap the tail into the mouth.

Bring the two 260s around the outside of the Linky balloon, crisscross them, and wrap the other tail of the Linky balloon into that spot to secure.

Twist a loop on each 260, starting from the crisscross point. Hide the nozzle of the Linky balloon.

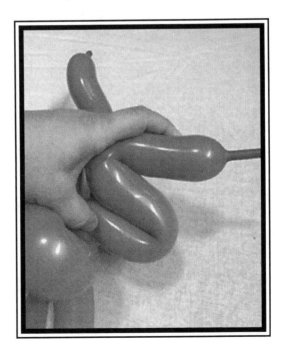

Bend and squeeze the ends of the 260s to shape the tail.

Measure along the top 260 about a hands width back from the lips and twist. Wrap the eyeball duplet into that point.

To See The Companion Video Go To:
https://youtu.be/mMbsDyEsuLY

Octopus

Materials:

- Four 260 balloons, fully inflated and burped
- One 11" balloon
- Two 5" eyeball balloons, tied in duplet

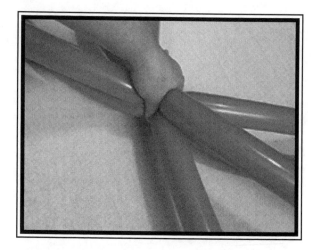

Hold four 260s together so that they are even. Squeeze in the middle and twist.

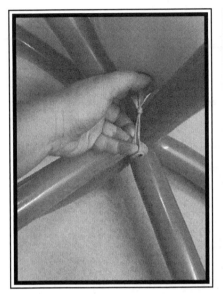 

Wrap the nozzle of the 11" balloon around the twist in the 260s.

Take the eyeball balloon duplet and twist it onto the octopus between the 11" balloon and the 260s.

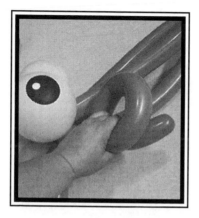

Shape the tentacles by gently curling the 260 around your hands and shifting the air by gently squeezing. Repeat on all eight legs.

To See The Companion Video Go To:
https://youtu.be/zkPb1R9g8SY

Sea Turtle

Inspired by a design by John and Johnna Perry

Materials:
- 2 260 balloons in 2 colors
- 5" balloon, white
- 160 balloon, inflated three quarters, matching one of the 260s

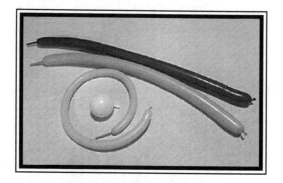

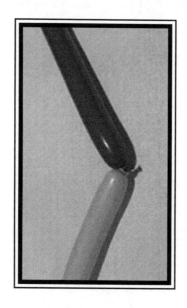

Start with two 260s, green and brown, inflated about three quarters. Tie them together into a duplet.

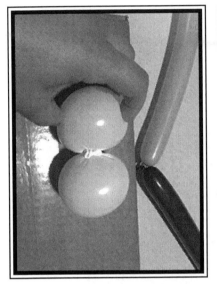 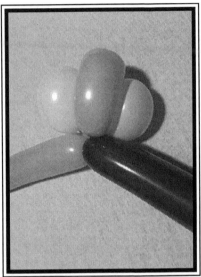

Inflate the white 5" balloon so that it is round, but very squishy. Split it in half and twist. Wrap the nozzle around the twist.

Starting at the point where you tied the duplet, wrap that green balloon around the round balloon bubbles and twist. These are your eyes.

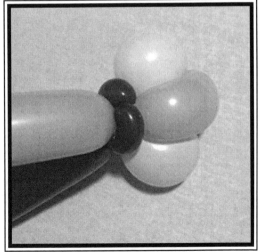

Take the brown (or purple) balloon and make two pinch twists to hold up the neck.

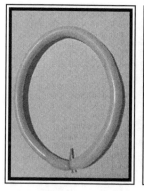 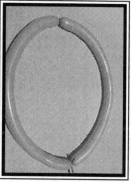 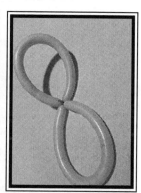

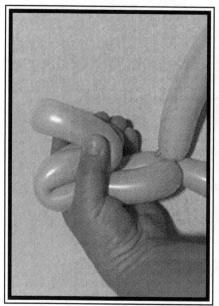 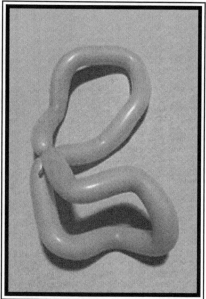

Take your 160 and tie it into a circle.

Find the center point across from the tie, pinch, and twist one side.

Collapse the circle so that the two twists meet and twist one side. Use any extra uninflated end to secure. You should have a figure eight shape.

You now want to give a little shape to the sides of your figure eight. Hold the circle together and gently squeeze into a Z. Repeat on both sides. These are your flippers.

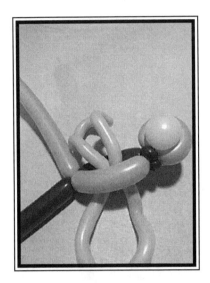
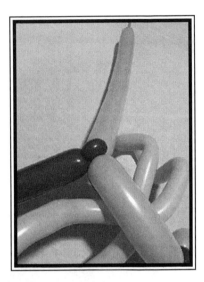
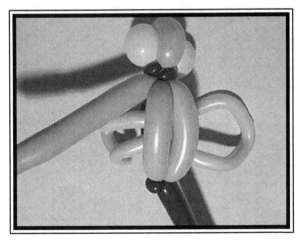

Place your flipper between the green and brown (or purple) 260s behind the eyes with the brown balloon on top. Twist a little behind the flippers to hold them in place.

Make a small pinch twist in the green balloon, and wrap it around, ending with the pinch twist and green balloon on the bottom.

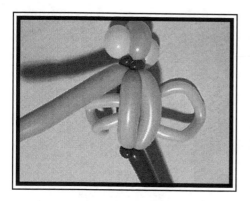

Bring the brown balloon up to the neck and twist. Bring it back down the back and twist. Bring it back up to the neck a final time and twist. You should have four equal bubbles along the back for your shell. Remove the excess brown balloon.

On the bottom, do the same with the green balloon, bringing it back and forth until you have three bubbles to create the belly.

Twist a small bubble at the end of the green balloon, bring it back up to the body to create a loop, and twist around the pinch twist.

Pinch the tail loop to split like you did the fins. Squish down so that the end of the tail loop meets the body, giving you two equal loops, and twist to secure.

Arrange the tail loops so that they are side by side.

Use a marker to draw on eyes, a nose, and a smile.

The DIY Balloon Birthday Bible

To See Companion Video Go To:
https://youtu.be/pQDRjm4VSn4

Seaweed Island

Materials:
- Four Agate balloons, blue
- Four Agate balloons, green
- Water weight
- Eight 260 balloons, shades of green

Tie Agate balloons into duplets of one green and one blue.

Twist two duplets together into a quad. Repeat with the other set of quads.

Twist the two quads together. Arrange, alternating blue and green. This will form a pocket on the inside where your water weight will rest.

Tie together green 260 balloons into duplets, matching shades. You should have four duplets.

Twist the 260 duplets together.

Attach the top of your water weight to the center of the cluster of 260 duplets using the nozzle. You want to tie it so that it still has some stretch.

Stretch the water weight so that most of the pull is on the neck above where it's tied. Wrap the water weight around the cluster of Agate balloons so that it rests in the pocket you created.

Play with the way the 260 balloons are arranged, crimping them to give a little bit of shape. Don't shape it too much, so that it stays natural looking and flowing. Have fun with it.

If you feel that it needs a bit more seaweed to fill it out, you can add in another 260 duplet.

If you are making a group of seaweed islands, use different shades of green and different colors so that they are not all exactly the same.

You can also make a short version by folding the 260s in half and twisting them together rather than creating duplets the full length.

Use sticky tabs to hide fish in the seaweed for extra fun.

To See The Companion Video Go To:
https://youtu.be/gZ6gh9RLaNY

NOTES

Life Preserver

Materials:
- Pex, plastic wire
- White 5" balloons, inflated to 4", tied in quads
- Red 5" balloons, inflated to 4", tied in quads

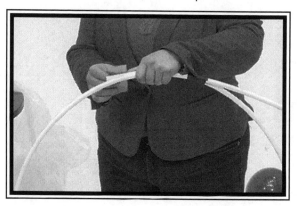

Make a circle out of your pex, overlapping the ends. Secure it with duct tape where needed. (You could also use a hula hoop, but this method is better if you want to control the size of the circle.)

Wrap your first white quad onto the pex circle. Continue, just like a column, stacking the balloons so that they nestle into each other. The pattern you're going to use is five white quads and three red quads.

Continue around the circle adding the quads in your pattern. The exact numbers of the quads are not as important as the ratio of red to white balloons. You can adjust the exact numbers to fit your circle.

To See The Companion Video Go To:
https://youtu.be/AB0GeMTlzig

NOTES

Anchor

Materials:
- Two aluminum rods, about 3' long
- Duct tape
- 5" round balloons, gold, inflated to 3", tied in quads
- One 5" round balloon, gold, inflated slightly larger than 3"
- 260 balloons, gold

Use duct tape to tape together the aluminum rods near the top and middle.

Bend the bottoms of the aluminum rods up at an angle to create an arrow shape. This is the frame for your anchor.

Use the duct tape to cover any sharp edges.

Take a 3" quad and twist it onto the frame at one of the bends you made. Pack quads along each of the lower sides that you created by bending the frame.

Once you have the bottom packed you are going to begin on the upright part of the frame.

Wrap the first quad at the base of the upright part of the frame so that it fits snugly against the balloons already on the frame. If you cannot get the fit you want, start with a duplet, and then continue packing with quads.

Pack quads up the frame until it is completely covered.

To create a tip on the bottom of your anchor, take a single gold round balloon and tie it to the bottom of your anchor right where the two bends meet.

Take a partially-inflated 260 balloon and make a loop. Tie it and deflate the end. Use the deflated end to tie the loop onto the top of the anchor. Make sure to weave the uninflated 260 down below the top cluster to secure.

To make the chain, start with two gold 260s and tie them together. Do the same with another set of gold 260s.

Put one 260 duplet through the loop at the top of the anchor, centering the knot on the loop. Twist the two 260s together to secure.

Nestle the second 260 duplet onto the twist you just made, and twist the other two 260s around it.

Continue alternating the duplet of 260s you twist around the other to make your chain link effect.

When you reach the end, twist all four 260s together. Put pinch twists at the end of each 260 to secure, and remove the excess balloon.

To See Companion Video Go To:
https://youtu.be/ezAH51aboKE

NOTES

Under the Sea Balloon Photo Frame

- With Caity Byrne, CBA
- Materials:
- Two lamp bases
- 10' of PVC, cut in half
- Two PVC corner connections
- Two PVC T connections
- Twenty-four 260 balloons, fully inflated, tied in duplets
- Thirty-six 5" round balloons, inflated to 3.5"-4", tied in groups of six
- Balloon anchor and/or balloon fish
- Balloon octopus
  Four 260 balloons, fully inflated and burped
  11" round balloon
  Two round eye balloons
- Sticky tabs

Attach the PVC to the lamp bases with the connections, using the corners at the top and the T connections at the middle. Make sure your connections are all taped securely. This creates your picture frame base.

Wrap two duplets of 260s together to create a quad.

Wrap the quad of 260s around the frame at the bottom corner where the PVC joins the lamp base.

Wrap the 260s up the lamp pole, two in the front and two in the back, and create the spiral as you go.

Once you get to the top corner, twist two of the 260s together. Wrap a third into that same point, and finish with the last one.

You can also create your 260 spiral by twisting together two 260s into a spiral and wrapping that spiral around the pole. Wrap the third and fourth 260s up the pole following the curve of the first two.

Attach another quad of 260s to the top corner where you stopped. Wrap across the top create your spiral just as you did with the first, stopping at the halfway point. Wrap them around each other and secure.

Continue with a third set of 260s across the second half of the top, creating your spiral until you reach the corner.

Repeat the same pattern of spiraled 260s around the entire frame.

Wrap a six pack of round balloons at each of the corners and the center points at the top and bottom to hide the joins and connections.

For extra decoration, use sticky tabs to attach a balloon anchor to the frame. You can also place seaweed islands in front of the frame and/or add some balloon fish.

To make a balloon octopus twist four 260s together at the center. Attach an 11" balloon at the same center twist. Tie two eyeball balloons into a duplet, and twist them between the 11" balloon and the 260s. Gently squeeze the 260s into a curl to give them shape. For more info, see chapters on the octopus, anchor, seaweed island and fish.

To See Companion Video Go To:
https://youtu.be/tfq48RXd5bU

Mini Palm Centerpiece

Materials:
- Four 11" round balloons, brown, tied in duplets
- Four 6.5" round balloons, brown, tied in duplets
- Base plate and pole
- Four 260 balloons, brown, fully inflated and burped
- Ten 260 balloons, green, fully inflated and burped.
- Three 5" balloons, yellow, inflated to different sizes

The size of your balloons will be determined based on whether you are creating a centerpiece or a standalone piece. For a centerpiece, start with 6" rounds, and the next set 4".

Twist two brown duplets together to create a quad. Wrap the quad onto the base of the pole.

Create a quad with the smaller set of duplets and wrap above the base quad.

Make a quad of brown 260s. Wrap the quad between the first and second round quads, so that one 260 balloon comes up between each round smaller balloon.

Twist two 260s together to create a spiral, and then wrap it around the pole. Twist onto the top of the pole to secure.

Wrap the other two 260s around the pole in same way to fill in the gaps and twist to the top.

To create the palm fronds, fold a green 260 in half and twist. Repeat with more green 260s, twisting them together in the middle to create a group. They don't have to be perfect.

Twist the group of green 260s to the top of the pole, using the extra brown balloon ends to secure it.

To remove the brown ends, deflate and wrap into the group. You can also leave them in if you like the look.

If you want to make your tree top fuller, you can add in more green 260s.

Tie the three yellow balloons together. Wrap the trio into the top of the tree so that it rests at the base of the green 260s like coconuts.

To See Companion Video Go To:
https://youtu.be/YIqbXJELmM8

NOTES

Palm Tree Balloon Tower

Materials:
- Base plate and pole
- 11" balloons, inflated to 6", tied in quads, orange/tan
- Ten palm frond balloons, inflated and tied in groups of five
- Three 11" balloons, brown, inflated to any size you like
- Uninflated 260

Begin wrapping your 6" orange quads at the base of the pole. Continue up the pole to the top.

Tie a group of palm frond balloons onto the top of the pole. Do the same with the second set of five on the other side.

Tie your three brown 11" balloons together. These will be your coconuts. Tie your uninflated 260 to the group. Attach under one set of palm fronds using the 260.

See The Companion Video, Go To:
https://youtu.be/lyUk7OdJUUo

Garden / Flower / Spring Theme

Fancy Butterfly

Materials:
- Five 260 balloons
- One 160 balloon

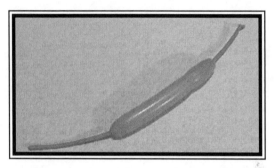

Start by prepping your 160. You want it inflated in the center. Stretch it a little bit back and forth to stretch out the center. Place the center in your mouth and suck a small bubble. Now put the 160 on the pump, and it will inflate in the center. You want about four or five inches in the center inflated. Tie off.

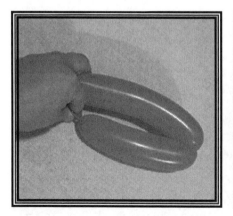

Take a 260. You are going to make an outside wing. Pick a size and make a dog leg. Twist two bubbles the same size, and then twist them together. Twist the nozzle and in and out to hold it.

Match those bubbles with a second set the same size. Sew the remaining end in and out to secure. Remove the excess.

Repeat the same thing with a second 260, making the bubbles smaller, about three quarters the size of the first set of wings. Remove the excess.

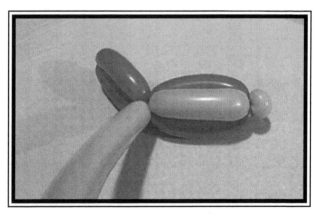

Take a third 260 and twist a small bubble. Use the nozzle to make a pinch twist.

Take your first set of wings and find the center point of one wing. Wrap the pinch twist of the third 260 at this point. Bring the third

260 along the wing and twist at the center to match the wing bubble size. Feed the end through a wing loop to secure.

Bring the third 260 across the other wing and twist a bubble the same size as the wing bubbles.

Twist a small bubble and pinch twist. Wrap the pinch twist through and around the wing to secure. Remove the excess.

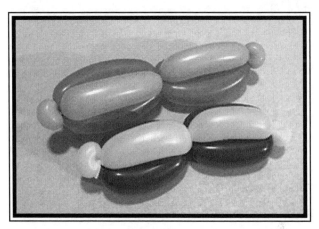

Take a fourth 260 and repeat the process with the second set of wings. Make a pinch twist and secure to the wing, match the wing bubbles, twist in the center, match the wing bubbles, make a pinch twist, and secure to the wing. Remove the excess.

Take your two sets of wings and twist them together at the center.

Arrange it so that you have an X shape with the single balloons on one side and the double wings on the other side.

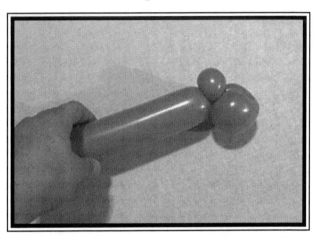

Take the final 260 and make a pinch twist. Twist a small loop for the head.

Use the wings to measure the length of the body bubble so the twist is right where the bottom wings meet. Twist.

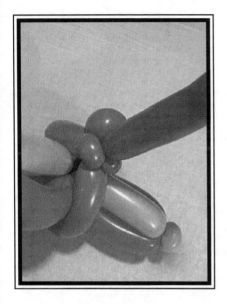 

Bring the final 260 up around the wings and twist around the head. Make a pinch twist and wrap around the head to secure. You should have two pinch twists at the head for small ears. Remove the excess.

Take the 160 you made earlier and twist it in half. Wrap the 260 in behind the ear twists and wrap around. Then bring the 160 up in front of the ear twists.

Squeeze a small amount of air up to the end of the 160 and tie off. Repeat on the second side. These are your antennae.

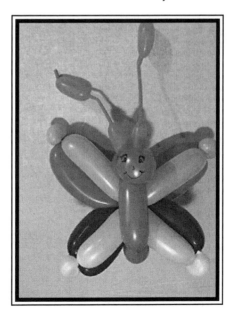

Use a marker to draw on a face.

You could also tie an uninflated 260 to the end of an inflated 260, and then tie the uninflated 260 to the butterfly behind the ears. Now you can make your butterfly fly.

See The Companion Videos Go To:
https://youtu.be/bviFWmb4L6g

Butterfly Cloud 9 Balloon Tower

Materials:
- Base plate and pole
- Butterfly mylar balloon
- Eight 11" balloons, inflated to 9", tied in quads
- Eight 11" balloons, inflated to 7", tied in quads
- Four 11" balloons, inflated to 5" tied in quads
- #4 wide ribbons tied in the middle

Wrap a 9" quad at the base of the pole. Wrap a 7" quad above that, and follow with a 5" quad.

Take another 9" quad and twist it onto the top of the pole. You can put an uninflated balloon over the very top of the pole to prevent anything sharp from popping the balloons and to give a better surface for your quad to grip.

Wrap a 7" quad underneath the 9" quad at the top of the pole.

Tie your butterfly mylar balloon to the top of the pole with an uninflated 260 balloon. Make sure the 260 is tied below the valve of the mylar balloon to prevent air from leaking out. Bring the 260 down below the 7" quad and tie, then weave the ends into the two upper quads.

Take your ribbons and tie them in below the 7" quad, weave the ribbon through the upper quads to secure.

Determine the length you want your ribbon to fall down the pole, fold it in half, and cut going down to create the V ribbon ends. You can use your scissors to give the ribbons some curl. You don't have to open your scissors; just apply the pressure against the flat edge.

o See The Companion Video Go To:
https://youtu.be/Y7H1D35vNcI

Giant Balloon Flower Pedestal

Materials:
- Base plate and pole, 3'
- Two 260 balloon, green, partially inflated
- Four 11" balloons, inflated to 8.5", green, tied in quad
- Four 11" balloons, inflated to 6", green, tied in quad
- Ten 11" heart balloons, tied in duplets
- Two 11" balloons, inflated to 6", yellow, tied in duplet

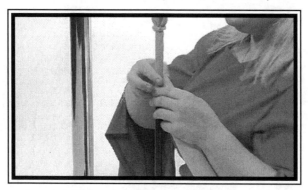

Tie the nozzle of the partially inflated green 260 and wrap it at the top of the pole. Wrap the 260 around the pole at an angle, covering the pole.

When you get to the end of the balloon maintain control and deflate the rest. While holding that end, bring the second partially inflated green 260 up above the end of the first and begin wrapping it around the pole. That will secure the end of the first balloon.

Continue wrapping down the pole until you reach the bottom. You don't have to go all the way to the bottom, because there will be quads at the base. Deflate the rest of the 260 and tie it around the pole.

Wrap the green 8.5" quad at the base of the pole. Wrap the green 6" quad above that.

Twist together all five duplets of 11" hearts. Arrange it so that there are five on one side and five on the other side.

Take the 6" yellow duplet and place it in the center of the heart group. Arrange it so that there are five heart balloons around each yellow balloon.

Place the flower onto the top of the pole. If you are going to be outside you may want to tie the flower on.

o See The Companion Video Go To:
https://youtu.be/RfsqpmXbd10

Balloon Flower Arch

Materials:
- 11" balloons, inflated to 7.5", tied in duplets
- 11" balloons, inflated to 6", tied in duplets
- Eight 11" balloons, inflated to 8", tied in quads
- Eight 11" balloons, inflated to 7", tied in quads
- Arch base, with center marked

To make the flowers, take five duplets of 7.5" balloons in one color and twist them together. Make a duplet of 6" balloons and bring it into the pack of 10 balloons to finish off the flower. Arrange so that you end up with a 6" balloon in the center of five 7.5" balloons on each side. This is your 12 balloon flower.

Start packing your arch in the center. You want to pull one of your flowers onto the arch at the center, so that the flower is facing out on each side.

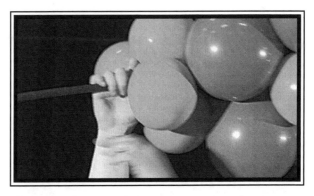

Take a 6" quad and wrap it onto the arch pole next to the flower. Wrap two quads on each side of the center flower.

Pull another flower onto the arch next to each pair of 6" quads.

Continue packing the arch with two 6" quads between each flower.

To finish the arch you are going to use the 8" and 7" quads. Wrap in the 7" quad followed by the 8" quad. Do the same on the opposite end of the arch.

o See The Companion Video Go To:
https://youtu.be/tQm7Y9le2mc

Baby Theme

Teddy Bear

Materials:
- One 260 balloon, inflated with a 5" tail

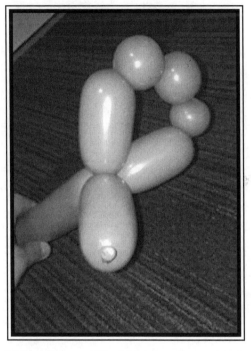

Using the 260, twist a soft bubble for the nose, about the length of your middle finger. Don't make it too small, because you're going to put another bubble into it later.

You are going to make a six bubble chain. Make sure you control the first bubble while making the next one.

Twist a bubble a little larger than your thumb, which will be a cheek.

Make a small 1" bubble for an ear. Make another small bubble for the forehead, and another 1" bubble for the second ear.

Now make another cheek bubble matching the size of your second bubble. As long as you control the first and last bubbles, your chain will stay twisted.

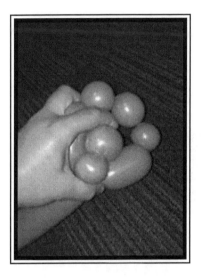 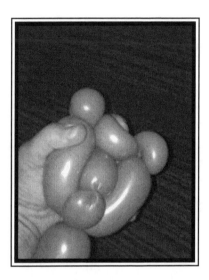

Lock your chain by twisting the first twist to the last twist.

Twist a small bubble at the base of your nose, and then push the nozzle end through the space between the cheek bubbles.

Hold the nose while pinch twisting both ear bubbles. Now you have the head.

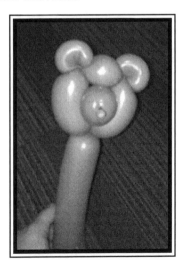 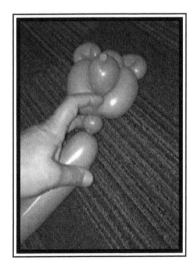

Twist a small bubble for the neck.

For the arms, twist about a 5" bubble. Match it with the next bubble and twist them together.

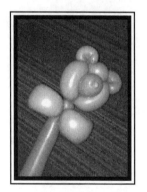 

Squish the connection point at the end of the arms toward the head and twist the two pieces. That makes the arms.

Twist a small bubble for the belly, like you did for the neck.

Now you're going to twist the legs, but make sure you leave a small bit at the end for a tail. Twist once for the first leg, bring the rest of the balloon up to match it and twist them together. Put the tail end in the back and leave the legs sticking out in front.

Do the same thing that you did with the arms. Push the connection point in towards the belly and twist.

See The Companion Video Go To:
https://youtu.be/CcHE5Jwazi0

NOTES

Pacifier

Materials:
- One 16" blossom or donut balloon
- One 11" balloon
- One 350 balloon

Tie the 350 balloon into a circle.

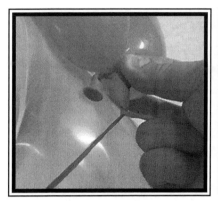
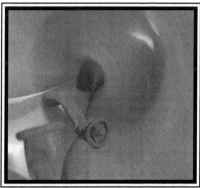

Pull the nozzle of the 11" balloon through the hole in the blossom balloon and hold it by the nozzle.

Tie the nozzle of the 350 circle to the nozzle of the 11" balloon.

If you were to helium fill the blossom balloon and the 11" balloon, your pacifier/rattle would float.

To See The Companion Videos Go To:
https://youtu.be/3wiXwtO3dWY

NOTES

Rubber Ducky

Materials:
- One 11" balloon, inflated about 7"
- One 260 balloon, inflated with a tail

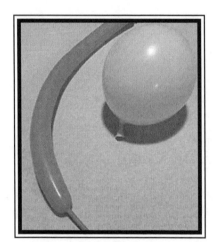
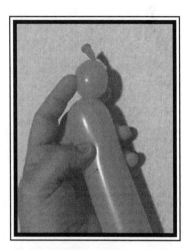

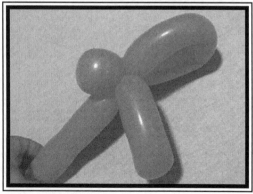

Hold onto your bubble while twisting the 260.
Twist a small bubble at the end of the 260.

Now make four loops; two small followed by two larger. Remove the excess 260.

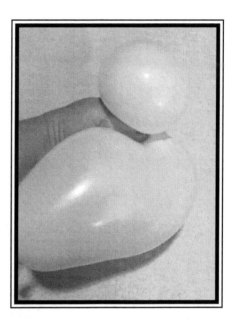

You are going to make a sidewall bubble in the 11" balloon. Squeeze the balloon toward the side, so that the air is pushing towards the neck of the balloon, and at the same time, twist a bubble.

Wrap your 260 around the bubble on the 11" balloon, arranging so that the first bubble sits in the back, the two small loops sit on the sides of the head like cheeks, and the larger loops are in the front for a beak.

Draw eyes on your duck with a Sharpie.

**To See Companion Video Go To:
https://youtu.be/_nf20pNHimU**

Baby Shower Teddy Bear Centerpiece

Materials:
- Eight 11" balloons, inflated to about 9", twisted into quads
- Base plate and pole
- Eight 11" balloons, inflated to about 5", twisted into quads
- Teddy bear mylar balloon
- Two 260 balloons, inflated into spirals
- Two 260 balloons, clear, inflated into spirals
- Four balloon teddy bears

Twist the 9" balloon quad onto the bottom of the pole.

Twist the 5" quad onto top of the 9" quad.

Now mirror on the top of the pole what you did on the bottom. Wrap the 9" balloons onto the pole at the top, and the 5" quad below that.

Tie an uninflated 260 to the nozzle of the mylar balloon, and use it to tie the balloon to the top of the pole. Crisscross the 260 in the top quads to secure it before tying.

Tie together the two 260 spirals. Wrap that duplet into the bottom of the centerpiece, between the two quads, so that the spirals stand up next to the pole.

Wrap one 260 spiral around the pole. Repeat with the second 260 spiral.

Tie the ends of the 260 spirals together. Slip the knot over one of the balloons from the top 5" quad to secure.

Take one of the clear 260 spirals. Fold it in half and insert it under two of the 5" balloons in the bottom quad.

Twist a small bubble on the clear 260 spiral and attach to the teddy bear tail bubble. Repeat on the other end of the clear 260. (* See Teddy Bear Chapter for instructions on Teddy Bear)

Repeat with the other clear 260 spiral on the top, folding it in half and inserting between the two top quads. Attach a teddy bear to each end.

The DIY Balloon Birthday Bible

To See The Companion Video Go To:
https://youtu.be/R8tSmHwerbc

Welcome Baby Balloon Pedestal

Materials:
- Water weight
- Nine 11" balloons, inflated to 9"
- Nine 11" balloons, inflated to 6"
- One 646 balloon, inflated with a small tail
- Mylar balloon
- Uninflated 260 balloon
- Three 260 balloons, partially inflated
- Five 5" balloons, inflated to 3", tied in a five pack
- Two 5" balloons, inflated to 1.5", tied in duplet

Create a duplet and a three pack with the 9" balloons and twist them together to create a five pack. Create another five pack with the 6" balloons.

Twist the two five packs together. Arrange so that the 6" balloons are all on the top.

Tie the water weight to the nozzle of the 646. Wrap this into the two five packs, so that the water weight goes into the pocket underneath the two five packs.

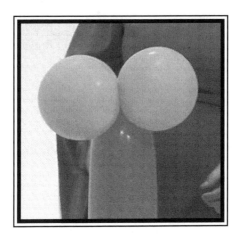

Create a quad with 6" balloons.

Push the air out of the top of the 646 and tie it to one of the nozzles of the 6" quad.

Create another quad with 9" balloons. Wrap it into the 6" quad at the top of the 646. Arrange so that the little balloons are on the bottom.

Tie an uninflated 260 onto the mylar balloon below the valve. Tie the mylar balloon onto the top of the column using the 260, figure 8 the ends around the quads to secure.

You don't want to use a really or heavy balloon at the top, because the base won't support it.

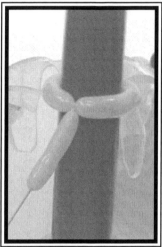

Take a 260 and wrap it around the column above the top five pack. Tie it securely and trim the ends. Do the same thing at the top below the smaller quad.

Wrap a third 260 around the center of the column and tie. Do not trim end.

Create a small flower by wrapping the 3" five pack and the 1.5" duplet together and arranging so that the duplet is in the center. Wrap the flower onto the center 260. Remove the excess 260. Deflate the back 1.5" balloon so that the flower will sit flatter.

See The Companion Video Go To:
https://youtu.be/IOGybXvyQ5o

Balloon Baby Bottle

Materials:
- Base plate and pole
- 11" balloons, inflated to 7", white, tied in six packs
- Six 11" balloons, inflated to 9.5", light purple, tied in six pack
- Five 11" balloons, inflated to 8", light orange, tied in five pack
- Four 11" balloons, inflated to 7", light orange, tied in quad
- Four 11" balloons, inflated to 5", light orange, tied in quad
- One 11" balloon, inflated to 6", light orange

To make the round shape of the bottle, you are going to use six packs to pack the pole. For this, you make three duplets and twist them together.

The first few six packs that you put on are going to fight with you, and you will have to make them go where you want.

Start wrapping a white 7" six pack at the base of the pole. Continue packing up the pole with white six packs almost to the top of the pole. Leave 1-1.5' at the top of the pole.

Take your 9.5" six pack and wrap it onto the pole above the white six packs. This is the lip of your bottle.

Wrap the 8" five pack on next.

Wrap the quad of 7" orange balloons on next.

Wrap the 5" quad onto next.

The single 6" orange balloon will be the bottle nipple. Tie it onto the top of the last pack that you put on the pole so that it stands in the center.

To See The Companion Video Go To:
https://youtu.be/CekUj_oDjfQ

General Décor

Birthday Balloon Totem Pole

Materials:
- Foil balloons, air filled
- Clear packing tape
- Base plate and pole

Tape down the tails of your foil balloons.

This is a design meant to be put against a wall. The back of the pole will be visible.

Start at the bottom of your pole. Tape your first foil balloon to the pole with clear packing tape. Repeat with another foil balloon, taping it securely to the pole.

Continue to the top of the pole, making sure that the pole is hidden from the front by the balloons.

You can add more balloons to the sides. Make a U out of your tape and attach it to the balloon you want to add. Then use the other part of the U to attach the balloon to the spot you want. Use more tape to reinforce it the connection and hold the balloon in the position you want. You could also use sticky tabs to add the balloons in.

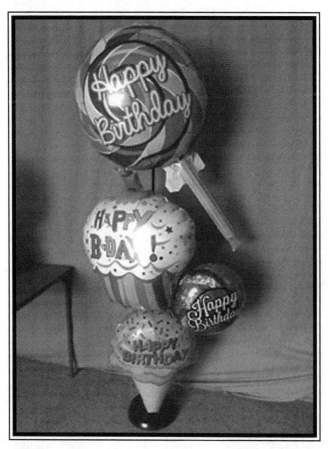

To See The Companion Video Go To:
https://youtu.be/8cZvsvxN6-A

Linky Arch

Materials:
- Two water weights
- Thirty-two 11" balloons, inflated to 10", quads
- Nine Linky balloons
- Thirty-two 5" balloons, inflated to 4.5", quads

Take two quads of 10" balloons and twist them together. You want a pocket to form at the bottom. Arrange the colors the way you want.

Tie an uninflated 260 to each water weight. Take one of the water weights and nestle it into the pocket at the bottom, wrapping the nozzle in among the round balloons to secure.

Take another 10" quad and place it above the base you created. Figure eight the uninflated 260 tied to the water weight around this third quad to secure.

The key to this arch staying together is that everything is very tight. Make sure to keep tension on the 260 as you attach new quads.

Attach a fourth quad to the stack, attaching with the 260. Figure eight the 260 through several times to secure and let it fall inside. This is one base of your arch.

Tie three Linky balloons into a tight chain.

Tie the chain of Linky balloons to the nozzle of one of the balloons in the top quad of your base.

Repeat this entire process to create a second base with a chain of three Linky balloons.

Create a third chain of three Linky balloons. Tie one end to the chain on the first base and the other end to the chain on the second base.

Your arch will be a bit floppy at this point. Twist a 4.5" quad between each Linky balloon to stabilize the arch.

You can create an arch with up to 11 Linky balloons and maintain stability. More than 11 Linkys, and you will need helium.

To See The Companion Video, Go To:
https://youtu.be/szumJ1juB6k

NOTES

Sandi Masori, CBA

Cupcake Balloon Tower

Materials:
- 11" balloons, rainbow colors, tied in quads
- Mylar cupcake balloon

The balloons in each quad should be the same color. You are going to make stripes of different colors as you go up the pole.

Wrap your first quad onto the bottom of the pole. Wrap a second quad on top of it, making sure the balloons nestle into each other rather than sitting directly on top of each other. Continue wrapping quads up the pole in the order you prefer.

Take your cupcake balloon and tie an uninflated 260 into a lark's head knot. Wrap the loop around the tail of the balloon and pull tight. The important thing is to make sure that your balloon is not tied directly over the opening where air goes in to prevent leaking.

Use the 260 to tie the cupcake to the top of the balloon column. Pull the ends of the 260 down on either side of the pole and crisscross into and around the second layer of 11" balloons. Tie. Crisscross down around the next layer of 11" balloons and tie again.

**To See Companion Video Go To:
https://youtu.be/ChRBsg9mcMg**

Zipper Pattern Balloon Tower

Materials:
- Base plate and pole
- 11" balloons, inflated to 8.5", four colors, tied in quads with one of each color
- Mylar balloon

Wrap the first quad at the base of the pole.

Wrap the next quad on like you are doing a spiral pattern. With the next quad you are going to match the color position of the first quad.

Continue wrapping the quads up the pole alternating the two positions to make your zipper pattern.

Use an uninflated 260 to tie the mylar balloon to the top of the pole. Tie it under the top two quads.

To See The Companion Video Go To:
https://youtu.be/agjs5Xxedjg

Birthday Number Guy

Materials:
- Giant foil number balloon
- Foil smiley face balloon
- Four 11" round balloons, inflated to 8.5", tied in quad
- Four 11" round balloons, inflated to 6.5" tied in quad
- Water weight
- Eight 5" round balloons, inflated to 4", tied in quads
- Four 11" round balloons, inflated to 6", tied in quad
- Sticky tabs
- Two 260s balloons, fully inflated
- One 260 balloon, inflated in a spiral

Twist together the 8.5" and 6.5" quads to make the base. Arrange so that the smaller quad is on top.

Tie an uninflated 260 to the bottom of the foil number balloon. Make sure to tie it under the valve. If the tab is very short you can use clear packing tape to tape down the valve and tape the 260 above it.

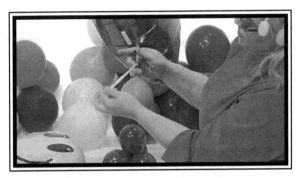

Tie the 260 to the water weight a short distance from the foil balloon.

Place the number balloon on top of the quad base and stretch the 260 so that the water weight fits into the bottom middle of the base.

Tie an uninflated 260 to the foil smiley face balloon. Tie the face balloon into the 6" quad.

Decide where you want the head and neck on your number balloon. Use stick tabs to attach the neck quad to the foil number balloon. Make sure you get the sticky tabs where the balloons connect.

Wrap an inflated 260 into one of the 4" quads. Make a bend for the elbow. Measure how long you want your arm to be and make a loop at the end for the hand. Use sticky tabs to attach the quad to the number balloon. Repeat for the second arm. Try to make them the same size.

Use sticky tabs to attach a spiraled 260 to the top of the foil smiley face balloon as a fun hat.

To See The Companion Video Go To:
https://youtu.be/t9gmd3Mt6E4

NOTES

Whimsical Cow

Materials:
- Four 11" balloons, inflated to 10", black, quad
- Four 11" balloons, inflated to 9", cow print, quad
- Water weight
- 3" balloon, white
- Cow head mylar balloon
- Four 11" balloons, inflated to 6", cow print, quad
- Sticky tabs
- Two 260 balloons, inflated with a tail, white

Twist together the 10" black and 9" cow print quads to make a big ball. Arrange so that cow print quad rests on top.

Place the water weight in the pocket that formed at the bottom of your ball. Stretch the nozzle up and figure-eight it through the balloons to secure. This is your base.

Tie the cow head to the white 3' balloon.

Take the 6" cow print quad and wrap it around where the cow head and 3' balloon connect. This will stabilize the head.

Place sticky tabs on the 9" cow balloons and place the 3' balloon on top to secure to base.

Tie together the two white 260s. Bend each 260 in half. It should look like an M.

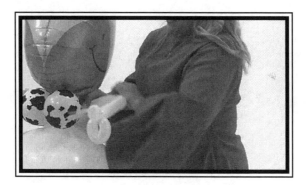

Squeeze the air down to the end of the 260s and twist a small bubble and a loop. Tie off. Repeat on the other 260.

Wrap the 260 duplet between the 6" cow print balloons and the 3' balloon, so that one sticks out on either side of the head.

Trim excess pieces.

To See The Companion Video Go To:
https://youtu.be/V2o9j6_e1r4

NOTES

Birthday Color Extravaganza Balloon Tower

Materials:
- Base plate and pole
- 9" balloons in eight colors
- Mylar balloon

Create two color sets for your balloons and tie into quads.

Take your first quad and wrap it to the base of the column. This will be color set A. Arrange in the color order that you want, because you will keep this order as you pack the pole.

Take a quad from color set B and wrap it directly above the first quad. Arrange the colors in the order that you want.

You are going to stack the pole alternating A and B quads. Make sure as you stack that you keep the same colors in the same places as you move up the pole.

Use an uninflated 260 to tie your mylar balloon to the top of the pole. Pull the 260 down and weave it under a few layers of the top quads and tie it in.

To See Companion Video Go To:
https://youtu.be/k4KufOMItls

Squiggle Surprise Pedestal

Materials:
- Base plate and pole
- 260 balloons, inflated in curlicues
- Nine 11" balloons, inflated to 7.5"
- Nine 11" balloons, inflated to 6"
- Water weight
- One 646 balloon, inflated with a 1.5" tail

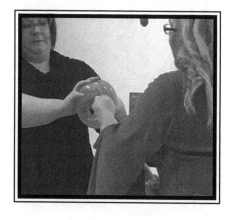

To create curlicues, start by fully inflating a 260 and then letting all the air out. Then wrap the 260 around your own fingers or a friend's, making sure not to twist it. Inflate the 260, making sure that you or your friend puts a little pressure on the 260 to keep it from falling off the fingers.

Make a five pack of the 7.5" balloons by twisting together a duplet and a triple (a duplet with a third balloon tied in.) Do the same with five 6" balloons.

Twist all 10 balloons together to make a giant ball. Arrange so that the 7.5" balloons are on the bottom, with the 6" balloons on top. Make sure there is a pocket on the bottom for the water weight to fit into.

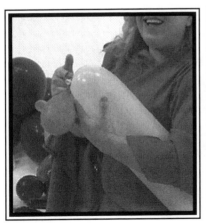

Tie the water weight to the nozzle of the 646, making sure to leave some slack.

Stretch the water weight and nestle it into the pocket at the bottom of your 7.5" five pack, with the 646 sitting in the top pocket formed by the 6" five pack.

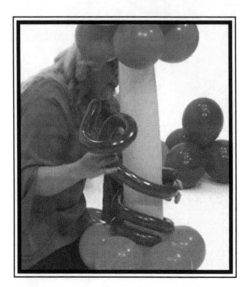

Create a quad of 6" balloons and wrap around the top of the 646, tying the tip of the 646 to the nozzle of one of the 6" balloons.

Make a quad of 7.5" balloons. Wrap one of the nozzles from the 6" quad around one of the 7.5" balloons and tie to a 7.5" nozzle. You should end with the two quads nestled on top of each other, mirroring the bottom.

Wrap a curlicue around the 646 starting at the bottom. Continue adding curlicues and wrapping up the 646, slightly overlapping them, until you reach the top of the 646. This will give some stability to your pedestal.

Tie curlicues together to create a duplet. Repeat with another two curlicues. Wrap the curlicue duplets together to create a quad. Continue adding duplets of curlicues until the group is as big as you want it to be.

Take an uninflated 260 and tie it into the middle of the curlicue group.

Place the curlicue group on top of your pedestal, and use the uninflated 260 to secure it to the top quads.

You may need to adjust to keep your pedestal from bending, depending on how many curlicues you have in your top.

To See The Companion Video Go To:
https://youtu.be/qVFk6DqscKU

Polka Dot Surprise Balloon Tower

Materials:
- Base plate and pole
- Twenty-four 11" balloons inflated to 6", tied in quad
- Twelve 11" balloons inflated to 9", tied in quad
- Four 260 balloons inflated in spirals
- Ten fully-inflated 260s with an inflated 5" balloon tied on each end

Wrap the 6" quad at the bottom of the pole. Wrap the 9" quad above that. Wrap another 6" quad on top of that.

Now you're going to do the top. Start at the very top with a 6" quad, wrap it around the pole. Wrap a 9" under that, and another 6" quad. It should mirror the bottom.

You are going to do the same thing in the middle of the pole. Start with the 9" quad and wrap it in the center of the pole. Wrap 6" quads above and below it.

Make sure all the balloons are nestling snugly against each other.

Tie together two spiraled 260s. Make sure they are spiraling in the same direction. Put them in underneath the top 6" quad of the middle group and arrange them so that they are sticking up next to the pole.

Take one of the spirals and wrap it around the pole, following the spiral. Do the same with the second one. Tie the two ends together and wrap it over one of the 6" balloons at the bottom of the top group to secure.

Do the same thing at the bottom, wrapping the spiraled 260s from the bottom of the middle group around the pole to the top of the bottom group.

Take one of the 260s with the 5" balloons on the end. Find the center and wrap in a second 260. Continue twisting in the 260s until you have a ball of all 10. It's okay if they're not exactly centered or even.

Take an uninflated 260 and wrap it around the center of your ball of 260s. You can put a little tie into it.

Put the ball on top of the column, and bring the uninflated 260 down and tie it into the group of quads at the top. Wrap it around and figure 8 it to secure. You want to tie it before you figure 8 it, because you don't want to put too much stress on the 260. You don't want it to snap.

Adjust the 260s at the top the way you like.

To See The Companion Video, Go To:
https://youtu.be/vmN1ayakKJU

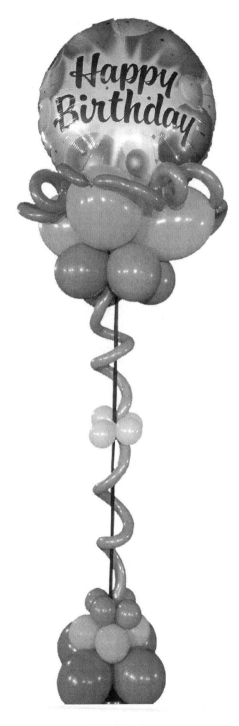

Electric Balloon Tower

Materials:
- Base plate and pole
- Eight 11" balloons, inflated to 8.5", bright blue, quads
- Eight 11" balloons, inflated to 5.5"-6", lime green, quads
- Four 5" balloons, inflated to 4", bright blue, quads
- Four linky balloons, fully inflated (12"), bright green, quad
- Six 260 balloons, inflated in curlicues, lilac
- Mylar balloon

Wrap a bright blue 8.5" quad onto the bottom of the pole.

Wrap a 6" green quad onto the pole next, followed by a 4" bright blue quad.

Next, wrap a quad of bright green linky balloons onto the top of the pole. Wrap an 8.5" quad of bright blue direction under the linky balloons.

Take a curlicue balloon and tie it into the 4" quad at the bottom of the pole. Wrap the curlicue around the pole.

Tie a second curlicue to the first and continue wrapping up the pole. Tie the end to the nozzle of one of the 8.5" quads at the top of the pole.

Wrap a 6" quad of lime green onto the middle of the pole where the curlicues are tied together.

Tie an uninflated 260 onto the neck of the Mylar balloon, being careful not to crush the valve.

Attach the Mylar balloon to the top of the column, figure eighting the uninflated 260 and tying to secure.

Tie together four curlicue balloons end to end.

Take the four curlicues that you tied together and tie them to the linky balloons between each curlicue. When you get to the end of your curlicue chain tie the ends together first, and then tie to the last linky balloon.

To See Companion Video Go To:
https://youtu.be/W6JaFqwzGP4

NOTES

Elegant Balloon Tower

By Caity Byrne, CBA
Beltway Balloons DC

Materials:
- Base plate and pole
- 8" balloons, white, quads
- 4" balloons, black, quads
- 3' balloon, black
- Four 260 balloons, fully inflated, white
- Sticky tabs

Begin packing the column with an 8" quad at the bottom.

Wrap a 4" quad above that, adjusting so that it nestles between the larger balloons.

Continue packing up the column, alternating quad sizes.

Take one of the white 260s. Attach sticky tabs to it. Begin attaching the 260 to the 3' balloon starting nozzle to nozzle. Attach one stick tab at a time to get your desired shape with the 260. Repeat around the 3' balloon with the other three 260s.

Attach an uninflated 260 the nozzle of the 3' balloon and secure to the top of the column.

To See Companion Video Go To:
https://youtu.be/a5EVn57YZlE

Out- Of- This- World Awesome Bouquet

Design Inspired by Ken Stillman

Materials:
- Water weight
- 260 balloons, inflated with a tail
- One 2 liter bottle, cut into about ¾
- Two Heart balloons
- 18" Mylar balloon
- 5" balloons (Alien Heads)

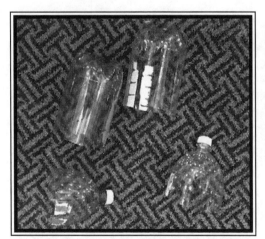

To make the stems: Take the nozzle of one of your 260s. You are going to use this to make some loops. Make your first loop and pull the nozzle through to secure. Keep your hold on the nozzle as you make the next two loops, wrapping the nozzle around each loop to secure.

Repeat this with 5-7 balloons. Try to make them about the same size. Save the tallest for the center.

Take the tallest one and tie it to the water weight.

You are going to use the 2-liter bottle as the base. Drop the water weight into it.

Take the rest of your stems and place them into the base with the first stem and the weight. Arrange them with shorter in front and taller in back.

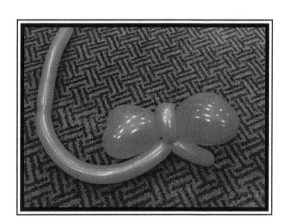

For the bow, make a duplet with two heart balloons.

Take a 260 that matches the color of your heart balloons. Twist off a bubble for the tail of your bow and hold it.

Wrap the 260 around where the hearts are joined and twist around your tail. This is your bow.

Wrap the long end of the bow around your stems in the base. You want it to be fairly tight so that it holds the first balloons together. Wrap the end of the 260 around the loop, not the hearts, to secure, leaving the tail hanging down next to the first tail.

If you want your bow tails to be the same length, twist the longer one so that it matches the first, deflate the excess and tie off.

Now you want to cover the base.

Twist a small bubble in a 260 and wrap it around the base of the 2 liter bottle and twist around the bubble to form a circle. Make it tight, but not so tight that it pops off the bottom.

Twist a small bubble to raise up a layer. Twist a bubble in the end of a second 260 and wrap it around the bubble in the first 260.

Bring your second 260 around the base to make a circle and twist both 260s to secure.

You want to go up another layer, so twist both balloons together to create two small bubbles.

Bring your first balloon around to create another circle around the base and twist.

Twist another small bubble, and bring the second balloon around the base in a circle.

When you no longer have enough of your 260s left to make a circle around the base, make a small pinch twist to secure.

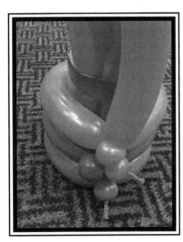

 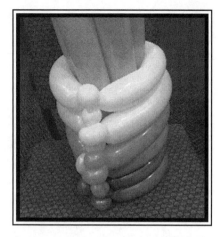

If you need more 260s to cover the base, twist a new one onto the pinch twist. Twist a bubble to go up, and wrap around the base. Continue until the base is covered. Secure with a pinch twist and remove excess and tie off.

Bend your balloon stems to give them some shape. Arrange so that the tallest is in the center.

Wrap the tail of your Mylar balloon into the center of the tallest stem, tucking the tail inside to hide it.

Tie alien head balloons onto the other stems.

Take another 260 the same color as your bow. Stretch it to make it a little thinner. Wrap it around the top of the base, securing to the bubbles on the back. Remove the excess and tie off.

Use scissors to trim off any excess ends

To See The Companion Video Go To:
https://youtu.be/qfbSWeGYmxw

Interactive Balloons

Maraca

Materials:
- Two sugar packets
- One 11" balloon
- Two 260 balloons, fully inflated and burped

Carefully pour two sugar packets into the 11" balloon. A funnel will make the process less messy.

Take one 260 balloon and tie it into a circle.

Find the midpoint of the balloon across from the tie, pinch it, and rotate one side.

Fold the 260 in half and twist. You should have a figure eight shape.

Fold in half at the twist, so you have a football shape. Take the nozzle and wrap it around the end to secure.

 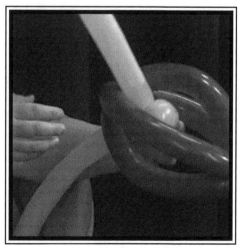

Take your second 260. Find the halfway point and twist.

Twist two small loops at the center.

Feed the 260 through your football shape until the two loops are in the center of the football. Flip both loops down so that they are on the outside of the first 260.

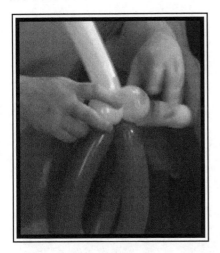 

Spiral the hanging ends of the second 260 together. Twist at the end and flip one through the spiral to lock.

Take your 11" balloon with the sugar and place it inside of the first 260. You are going to inflate it inside of the 260 so that you don't make it the wrong size.

Carefully use a pump to inflate the 11" balloon until it just fills the 260 surrounding it. Very careful tie it off.

Gently rotate the 11" balloon so that the nozzle is at the bottom, and wrap it around the 260s to secure.

To See The Companion Video Go To:
https://youtu.be/t3AZ0wlbCMM

NOTES

Balloon Instrument

Materials:
- One 11" balloon
- One 260 balloon
- One 260 balloon scrap

Tie three knots in the tail end of the 260 balloon in the same place, so that you get one big knot.

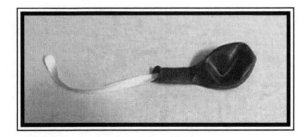

Feed the knot into the 11" balloon until you can feel it at the bottom.

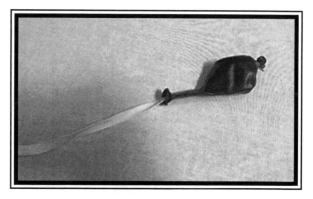

Wrap your 260 scrap around the bottom of the 11" balloon so that it captures the knotted 260 inside the 11" balloon. Tie off.

Turn the 11" balloon inside out.

Inflate the 11" balloon so that it is a little squishy. Tie off.

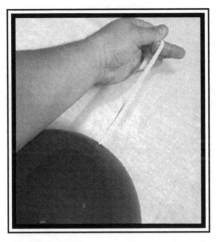

To play, hold the 11" balloon stable either under your arm or between your legs. Pull the 260 tight and strum. The length and tightness of your 260 will determine your pitch.

To See The Companion Video, Featuring Kat McDowell, Go To: https://youtu.be/7PIPVHEZ1oQ

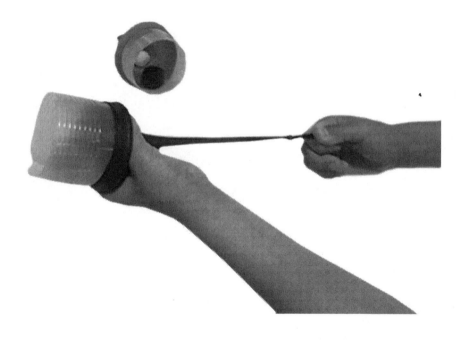

Marshmallow Shooter

Materials:
- 9 oz. plastic cup with the bottom third cut off
- 11" balloon

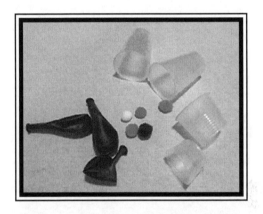

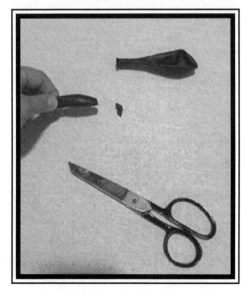

Cut the tip off the 11" balloon.

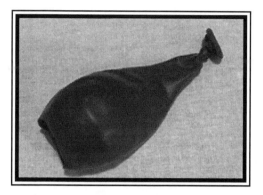

Tie a knot in the 11" balloon towards the middle.

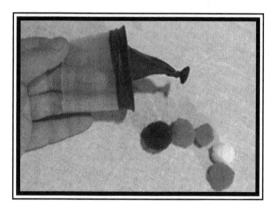

Put your fingers in the hole where you cut off the tip and stretch it over the plastic cup. You want it down over the lip, but not so close that it will pull off.

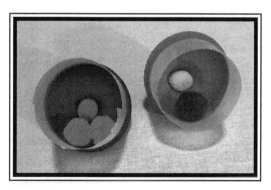

To fire, put a handful of marshmallows into the cup. Pull down on the nozzle of the balloon, and let it go to shoot.

To See The Companion Video Go To:
https://youtu.be/EQqWFWfzWQI

Who Is Sandi Masori?

Sandi Masori, who has been called "America's Top Balloon Expert" and "The Martha Stewart of Balloons" by the media, wears many hats (no pun intended).

Sandi, former elementary school teacher and a veteran of the balloon industry since the early 1990s, was the first female balloon "twister" to put out an instructional video for the balloon industry. Since then, she has gone on to make a LOT of local and national TV appearances (at the time of this writing, 62 and counting), and several hundred "how to" videos on her Sandiballoon YouTube channel. She's one of the original "deco- twisters", moving fluently between balloon decorations and balloon twisting, and often combining them together.

She's become one of YouTube's "creators," having built up her following enough to become part of the YouTube Space program, and now shoots many of her videos in their studios.

Masori is also the author of the best-selling books: *The DIY Balloon Bible for All Seasons, The DIY Ballon Hat Bible, The Event Planners Essential Guide to Balloons,* and *The Ultimate Guide to Inflating Your Trade Show Profits... With Balloons!*

Since the year 2000, she has run Balloon Utopia (http://www.BalloonUtopia.com), San Diego's premier balloon event décor and entertainment company, serving the corporate and high-end markets.

She also runs The Balloon Expert School, (http://www.BalloonExpertSchool.com), teaching emerging balloon artists how to build and run their balloon business.

While she's doing all of that, she's also a devoted mother, and daughter.

In her spare time, she enjoys hanging with family, reading, traveling and exploring new Sushi restaurants.

Who Is Caity Byrne?

Before she was Twister-in-Chief to Beltway Balloons, Caity Byrne was the Editor-in-Chief for several medical, technical, and fictional publications for both non-profit and corporate organizations. Her own work has been published in everything from trade magazines to peer-reviewed medical journals. With an eagle eye and gusto for grammar, she will always be an editor, but balloon art is her true passion. From humble beginnings with a how-to book (far less detailed than this one,) Caity has grown to become Washington DC's Top Balloon Decorator 2015 (thumbtack.com) and has won several awards for her twisted balloon creations. She runs Beltway Balloons full time and enjoys spending her free time reading in the company of her incredible husband, Matt, and their two fur babies, Noodles and Slartibartfast. See what she's up to at www.BeltwayBalloons.com

Thank You

Thank you so much for reading my book. We hope you have found value in it. If you have any questions, send us an email and let us know. Sandi@BalloonUtopia.com

Subscribe To My You Tube Channel – Http://www.YouTube.com/Sandiballoon

Check Out My Other Books- http://www.amazon.com/Sandi-Masori/e/B008ETA9RS

Join our Facebook community, ask your questions and show us your stuff! Http://www.facebook.com/groups/DiyBalloonArt

WANT MORE??? Special bonus – 12 more recipes/ chapters! Go to http://bit.ly/diyBdayBonus

Made in the USA
San Bernardino, CA
25 June 2016